"Christians believe the Scriptures to be authoritative. But what would justify this belief, especially if the Scriptures themselves contain numerous errors and morally problematic views? In this wonderfully accessible yet sophisticated book, Steve Layman addresses this question head-on: the Scripture's authority is grounded in Christ's authority. The discussion both stimulates and sparkles. I am so impressed by how much it accomplishes in so few pages."

—**TERENCE CUNEO**, Marsh Professor of Intellectual and Moral Philosophy, University of Vermont

"What exactly do we mean when we claim that the Bible is divinely inspired and why do we believe it truly is the word of God? In this superb study, Steve Layman carefully examines all the major views. I have never read a discussion as clear and philosophically informed. No matter what your position, you will achieve new clarity and depth if you read this excellent book by a first-rate Christian philosopher."

—**PAUL HERRICK**, Professor of Philosophy, Shoreline Community College

"Despite the unquestionable import of Christianity's commitment to the authoritative status of the Bible, perhaps few everyday Christians are familiar with the arguments for and against assigning it this status. In *Is the Bible the Word of God?*, Layman addresses this deficit by carefully reproducing, in his characteristically lucid prose, the key tenets of the debate in a way that is simultaneously illuminating and accessible."

—**REBEKAH L. H. RICE**, Professor of Philosophy, Seattle Pacific University

"What does it mean when Christians call the Bible the word of God? Given the many troubling passages in the Bible (such as commands to murder innocent people, prophecies that remain unfulfilled, and passages that seem to conflict with other passages), how can it make sense to claim that a good God stands behind such passages? Further, how does that claim fit with the statement in the Gospel of John that Jesus is the Word of God? Layman squarely faces many of the problems Christians face in calling the Bible the word of God, while also calling attention to the moral beauty of many biblical teachings. In the end, Layman argues that the Bible is generally reliable and that we should interpret the Bible according to the principles of love and justice. If you want to confront some of the toughest questions at the heart of Christian belief in the Bible, led by a thoughtful guide, then this book is for you."

—**RONALD FEENSTRA**, Professor of Systematic Theology, Calvin Theological Seminary

Is the Bible the Word of God?

Is the Bible the Word of God?

An Essay on the Authority of the Bible

C. STEPHEN LAYMAN

WIPF & STOCK · Eugene, Oregon

IS THE BIBLE THE WORD OF GOD?
An Essay on the Authority of the Bible

Copyright © 2025 C. Stephen Layman. All rights reserved. Except for brief quotations in critical publications or reviews, no part of this book may be reproduced in any manner without prior written permission from the publisher. Write: Permissions, Wipf and Stock Publishers, 199 W. 8th Ave., Suite 3, Eugene, OR 97401.

Wipf & Stock
An Imprint of Wipf and Stock Publishers
199 W. 8th Ave., Suite 3
Eugene, OR 97401

www.wipfandstock.com

PAPERBACK ISBN: 979-8-3852-6006-5
HARDCOVER ISBN: 979-8-3852-6007-2
EBOOK ISBN: 979-8-3852-6008-9

VERSION NUMBER 11/12/25

Scripture quotations are from *New Revised Standard Version Bible* (NRSV), © 1989, the Division of Christian Education of the National Council of Churches of Christ in the United States of America.

Scripture quotations are from *The Holy Bible English Standard Version* (ESV), © 2001, by Crossway, a publishing ministry of Good News Publishers. ESV edition 2016. Used by permission. All rights reserved. The ESV text may not be quoted in any publication made available to the public by a Creative Commons license.

Scripture quotations are from *The Holy Bible*, New International Version (NIV), © 1973, 1978, 1984 by International Bible Society.

Contents

Preface | vii
Acknowledgements | ix
Introduction | xi

1. Clarifying Key Concepts | 1
2. Revelation in Christian Perspective | 4
3. Our General Epistemic Situation | 7
4. The Bible Itself as Evidence? | 10
5. Obstacles (Old Testament) | 12
6. Obstacles (New Testament) | 23
7. Curley's Illuminating Reductio | 27
8. A Popular Solution Fails | 30
9. God's Thoughts Are Higher Than Ours | 34
10. Killing and Moral Theology | 36
11. Three Approaches to Biblical Interpretation | 42
12. W. J. Abraham's Approach | 49
13. Reformed Epistemology | 53
14. Swinburne's Approach | 60
15. Prophecy and Biblical Authority | 71
16. Messianic Prophecy | 82

Contents

17 Curley's Reductio Revisited | 89
18 Summary of the Case for Biblical Authority | 96
19 Problematic Divine Commands | 109
20 Problematic Passages on Moral Issues | 113
21 The Problem of Hell | 119
22 Epilogue | 127

Appendix: In Vitro Fertilization and the Right to Life | 131
Works Cited | 143
Index | 147

Preface

FOR MANY CHRISTIANS, THE *Bible is the word of God* is the fundamental theological claim. And on that fundamental claim, all their theological and moral thinking is based.

But strangely, *the Bible is the word of God* often operates as an unsupported assumption—as "a matter of faith," as some would put it.

Obviously, however, any religious group could adopt a book as "the word of God" and base their theological and moral thinking on it. Why the Christian Bible, which combines the Old and New Testaments? Why not the Hebrew Bible? Or the Qur'an? The Upanishads? The Zoroastrian Avesta? Why think *any* of these books is divinely inspired, or authoritative, or a written revelation? Surely, taking any book as the word of God, apart from evidence or philosophical vindication, is a dubious practice. Such a practice does not *rightfully* secure belief, though it apparently often does.

Furthermore, when we look into the reasons that are sometimes given for believing that the Bible is the word of God, we find much that is highly questionable. And we quickly realize that it is no small task to justify the claim that the Bible is divinely inspired, or authoritative, or a written revelation.

Additionally, in attempting to locate a credible justification for regarding the Bible as (in some sense) a message from God, we are forced to consider divergent approaches to biblical interpretation.

PREFACE

And in doing so, I shall maintain, we uncover profound deficiencies in some common ways of interpreting the Bible.

In the pages that follow, I have tried to offer a clear and honest discussion of the Bible as a message from God. Too often, in my estimation, Christian thinkers do not confront the relevant problems with intellectual honesty. For example, the very content of the Bible is a major obstacle to any defense of the claim that it is the word of God. Easy solutions are offered, and often accepted, but I will argue that they do not hold up under scrutiny.

I write in the belief that Christians of all denominations would benefit from a careful evaluation of their acceptance of the Bible as divinely inspired, as authoritative, and/or as a written revelation. Such an evaluation has a bearing on how Christians defend their faith, and, I shall argue, it has important implications for how they interpret the Bible, including how they interpret biblical passages regarding moral issues.

Acknowledgements

I WISH TO THANK Jerry Carter, Bill Custer, and Paul Herrick for insightful comments on earlier drafts of this work.

Introduction

CHRISTIANS IN GENERAL, INCLUDING Christian scholars, support their views by appealing to the Bible. But the appeal to the Bible makes sense only if one reasonably believes that the Bible is a reliable authority. Of course, Christians think the Bible is a reliable authority because they think it is the word of God, or divinely inspired, or a divine revelation.

But often there is no felt need to provide reasons or grounds for thinking that the Bible is a reliable authority (or divinely inspired, or a message from God, or a revelation). As philosopher-theologian William J. Abraham observes, many believers "simply hold to it [the Bible as a divine revelation] as a matter of faith; that is, they believe in divine revelation without evidence."[1]

Of course, most philosophers would agree that many beliefs do not need to be based on other beliefs to be rational or warranted. Such beliefs are said to be *properly basic*. For example, everyone or virtually everyone believes that *trees exist* and that *other people exist*, but not on the basis of arguments (i.e., other beliefs). Such properly basic beliefs are presumably somehow grounded in sense experience, and so they are rational or warranted. Could *the Bible is the word of God* be properly basic? We will consider such

---

1. Abraham, *Crossing the Threshold*, 2.

a view in due course, but for now, I'll simply note that it would be important to explain *how* such a belief could be properly basic.

The general structure of theological reasoning for many Christians seems to be this:

1. The Bible is the word of God. (Unsupported assumption)
2. The Bible says that X (where X is a statement or proposition, such as *Jesus is Lord*).
3. So, X.

But *merely assuming* that the Bible is authoritative—that it's the word of God, or divinely inspired, or a revelation from God—is plainly a questionable practice. After all, any religious group could write a book and make a baseless claim to the effect that the book is divinely inspired or divinely authorized. If the Christian has no good reason to regard the Bible as reliable or authoritative, then why rely on the Bible as opposed to, say, the Qur'an or the Upanishads? Is the decision to rely on a sacred text like tossing a coin? Surely the decision is much too important for that.

Are there any good reasons or grounds for thinking the Bible is the word of God (or divinely inspired or a revelation)? If an argument is not needed, why not? Also, does the attempt to vindicate one's belief in the authority of the Bible (with or without an argument) have implications for how one interprets the Bible? These are the questions I shall take up.

1

Clarifying Key Concepts

REVELATION IS DISCLOSURE, MAKING something manifest that was hidden. God may reveal truths to humans through various means, for example, through the experience of nature (e.g., the starry night sky), through conscience, through dreams and visions, through miracles, as well as through the written word. By contrast, to claim that the Bible is *divinely inspired* is to claim that God gave the human authors thoughts or guided their thoughts *directly* (miraculously). Of course, if the Bible is divinely inspired, then presumably it reveals truths to human beings—to those who read it, hear it read, hear sermons based on it, and so on. But inspiration and revelation are distinct concepts. And so, *conceivably*, the Bible could reveal important theological truths without being divinely inspired. (More on this momentarily.)

To speak of the Bible as infallible or inerrant is to say roughly that it is without error when correctly interpreted—without error at least as originally written (some errors may have been introduced as copies were made). While many assume that if the Bible is divinely inspired, it is without error, this assumption is by no

Is the Bible the Word of God?

means obviously correct. For example, it might conceivably fulfill God's purpose to communicate certain *important* truths, and that purpose might allow for some falsehoods to creep into the text because of the limitations and biases of the human authors.

Here it is well to keep in mind that we humans constantly appeal to authorities that are fallible. We routinely use dictionaries, textbooks, encyclopedias, maps, works of history, news reports, doctors' diagnoses, and so on. It is perfectly reasonable to appeal to such authorities, even though we know they sometimes include or involve errors. In fact, *most of what we know*, we know through fallible human authorities.

Written or spoken words might be a message from God (and hence, in some sense, God's *word*), even if they are not inspired by God. Consider, for example, the phenomenon of *appropriated* speech or writing. Philosopher Nicholas Wolterstorff has emphasized its potential relevance for understanding how the Bible, or parts of it, might be understood as a message from God.[1] Suppose Jack and Jill are at a committee meeting in which a controversial issue is being discussed. Jill gives a short speech summarizing her view of the matter. The committee chair asks Jack for his opinion. Jack simply replies, "I agree with Jill" or "My view is much the same as Jill's." Jack has *appropriated* Jill's speech, her message to the group. Similarly, God might conceivably appropriate the words of a human author whose message he (God) approves of. And conceivably some books of the Bible are books God has *appropriated* by means of the church's including those books in the canon of Scripture.

As Wolterstorff has observed, God might also speak through some humans by letting them serve as deputies. A deputy is authorized to speak in the name of another. Thus, an ambassador may be given the task of conveying a message for the president or prime minister. And a deputy may use her own words and ways of speaking (or writing) in conveying a message. Some biblical prophets might be regarded as deputies chosen by God.

---

1. For Wolterstorff's discussion of appropriated speech and deputized speech, see his *Divine Discourse*, 42–54.

Clarifying Key Concepts

In my view, to say that the Bible is the word of God (or a message from God) is not necessarily to say that it is divinely inspired or infallible (or inerrant). The claim that the Bible is the word of God (or a message from God) is, in my view, best understood as the claim that the Bible is *authorized* (or approved) ultimately by God—perhaps indirectly through the church—for certain purposes, among them the purpose of conveying key truths about how humans can be rightly related to God. The apostle Paul provides a broader list of purposes: "All Scripture . . . is useful for teaching, for reproof, for correction, and for training in righteousness, so that everyone who belongs to God may be proficient, equipped for every good work" (2 Tim 3:16-17 NRSV).

While I have drawn distinctions between the claims that the Bible is inspired, or God's word, or a revelation, I think these varying expressions are normally understood to imply that the Bible is a divinely authorized (or approved) source of truths concerning God and what God requires of human creatures. And this is the issue I wish to address.

2

Revelation in Christian Perspective

FROM THE STANDPOINT OF traditional Christian theology, the central revelation of the Christian faith is not the Bible. The central revelation is the incarnation: a divine person, the eternal Son, became a human being, "became flesh and lived among us" (John 1:14 NRSV). The earliest disciples, especially those we call apostles, witnessed the incarnation firsthand. They walked with Jesus of Nazareth, listened as he spoke, taught, argued, and preached; witnessed his actions (such as cleansing the temple and healing the sick); witnessed his crucifixion and death; and were present at his resurrection appearances. Jesus himself (his words, actions, example, death, and resurrection) is the central revelation, according to historic Christian theology. The apostles didn't read about this; they witnessed it. (Note: in this paragraph and the next I am simply stating the traditional Christian perspective, which includes the belief that the gospels give at least a generally accurate account of the teaching, actions, death, and resurrection of Jesus of Nazareth. Of course, nowadays many would deny that the gospels are reliable historical documents. I examine this denial in chapter eighteen.)

Revelation in Christian Perspective

"Jesus said to him, 'Have I been with you so long, and you still do not know me, Philip? Whoever has seen me has seen the Father. How can you say, *Show us the Father?*'" (John 14:9 ESV). Simply put, from the traditional Christian perspective, if you want to know what God is like, learn about Jesus of Nazareth. In his character, teachings, and actions, we have a revelation of what God is like. This is the central revelation of the Christian faith.

But we only know about Jesus from the New Testament writings, especially the gospels, so don't Christian claims about the incarnation—about Jesus' life, teaching, actions, and so on—depend on the claim that the gospels are divinely inspired? Not necessarily. At least in principle, the gospels might simply be writings based on eyewitness accounts of Jesus' actions, teaching, death, and post-resurrection appearances. The writers might *in principle* be no more inspired than a contemporary biographer of, say, George Washington or Marie Curie. It is not the words of the gospels, but the reality behind the words—Jesus' actions, teaching, death, and resurrection—that is the central revelation of the Christian faith.[1]

Consider that the first generation of Christians did not have the New Testament. It was in the process of being written. So, *The Bible is the word of God*, where the Bible includes the New Testament, is not a belief the very earliest Christians could have had. But they did possess the central Christian revelation, either directly (in the case of the apostles and other eyewitnesses of Jesus' life and teaching) or indirectly through the preaching and teaching of the apostles (and other eyewitnesses).

Many Christian theologians see further sources of revelation in the ecumenical creeds, such as the Nicene Creed, and in the lives of the exemplary saints. Too often the issue of divine revelation is reduced to the question whether the Bible is divinely inspired or authorized. The question "Have we (humans) been given a divine

---

1. Note: there are a few references to Jesus in first-century writings outside of the New Testament. For example, there are brief references to Jesus in the works of the Roman author Tacitus and the Jewish historian Josephus. But without the New Testament writings, and especially the gospels, we would know very little about the life and teachings of Jesus. See Bruce, *New Testament Documents*, 100–120.

revelation?" is much broader than the question "Is the Bible a divinely inspired (or divinely authorized) book?"

And yet, as philosopher Richard Swinburne points out, "There has been a strain in Protestantism, with its immense reverence for Scripture, to write of the Holy Scripture itself as the original revelation; what was given by God was the Bible."[2] It is this strain of thought that I am here trying to correct. From the standpoint of traditional Christian theology, the original revelation is Christ himself—his teaching, actions, death, and resurrection. That said, Christians do of course view the Bible as authoritative—as a message from God, as divinely inspired, or as a divine revelation. And in this work, I am focusing on whether and how such views can be justified or vindicated (if at all).

---

2. Swinburne, *Revelation*, 136.

3

Our General Epistemic Situation

FROM THE PERSPECTIVE OF an atheist, the Bible obviously contains a lot of unbelievable content, for example: (a) all the miracle stories and (b) all the thus-saith-the-Lords in the Old Testament. From an atheist's point of view, there is obviously no God to work miracles and no Lord God to issue commands. So, the claim that *the Bible is the word of God* presupposes that we can know or at least reasonably believe that God exists.

And it must be understood that the God of Christian theology is both almighty and loving. While a detailed discussion of these divine attributes is not needed for present purposes, a brief note about each of them may help to ward off some potential misunderstandings.

If God is almighty, there is no state of affairs that God is unable to bring about *due to a lack of power*.[1] But most Christian theologians would agree that God cannot make logical contradictions true, for there is no such thing as a *power* to make contradictions

---

1. This definition is a paraphrase of one offered by Wielenberg, "Omnipotence Again," 42.

true (e.g., that God exists and simultaneously does not exist). On the other hand, an almighty God can perform wonders—create the universe ex nihilo (out of nothing), stop a tornado in its tracks, cure cancer, and raise the dead.

It will be sufficient for present purposes to note just one aspect of love. If we love someone, we care about her long-term best interests. The phrase "long-term" is crucial here. A parent who loves a child may treat the child rather harshly in the short-term, for example, by "grounding" her or denying privileges. Similarly, the love of God can at times be so-called "tough love." We might call it *holy love*. God is not our indulgent grandfather who art in heaven.

The claim that an almighty, loving God exists is a major metaphysical thesis, subject to well-known objections, such as the problem of evil: "Would a loving God allow all the evil and suffering we find in the world?"[2] Another major objection is the problem of divine hiddenness, roughly: "If a God of love existed, he would make his existence known to everyone, but that hasn't happened, so there is no God of love."[3]

Discussions of God's existence certainly do not settle the issue *in the sense of* either (a) persuading everyone that God exists or (b) showing that non-theists (in general) are unreasonable.[4] Given all the evil and suffering in the world, it is understandable that many find it hard to believe in a God who is both almighty and loving. This leads to an observation that is very important for present purposes. *Assuming God exists, God apparently is not in the business of making the single most important theological truth— namely, "God exists"—clear to one and all, or undeniable, or obvious.* And if that is so, why should we expect matters of theology in general to be clear to one and all or obvious? We shouldn't. And if

---

2. For a rigorously formulated version of the problem of evil, see Rowe, "Problem of Evil," 335–41.

3. For carefully crafted statements of the problem of divine hiddenness, see Schellenberg, *Divine Hiddenness and Human Reason* and also Schellenberg, *Wisdom to Doubt*.

4. For a detailed discussion of God's existence, including the problems of evil and divine hiddenness, see Layman, *God*, 1–125. See also Herrick, *Philosophy, Reasoned Belief, and Faith*.

we are expecting the issue of biblical authority to be easily resolvable, our expectations are not well grounded. We are bound to be disappointed.

In general, large-scale philosophical and theological claims cannot be settled decisively. Multiple points of view can usually be defended *reasonably*.

Then why bother to reason about such things? First, some views are clearly more defensible than others. If we are rational, we try to locate the most defensible view or views. Second, some views are not defensible. Or at least they are extremely problematic. Surely, we should reject these views. Third, we can often learn a lot by thinking philosophical and theological issues through, even if, in the end, we cannot locate decisive arguments in the sense of arguments that persuade everyone or show those who disagree to be irrational.

Now, for present purposes, I'm assuming that the preliminary issue of God's existence can be resolved in favor of belief. Even with this assumption, however, it is still no trivial task to defend the belief in the authority of the Bible.

4

The Bible Itself as Evidence?

COULD THE CONTENT OF the Bible itself count as evidence (at least partial evidence) for the belief that God exists and has revealed truths to humans? Or at least for the belief that it *might well be true* that God exists and has revealed truths to humans? In principle, I think so. For example, if the content of the Bible were *just the sort of message we would expect a loving God to convey to his creatures*, that content might serve as partial evidence for God's existence. As philosophers Sandra Menssen and Thomas Sullivan have noted, "Inquirers are looking for a revelation that gives good guidance for conduct, instruction about how to become intimate with God and others, how to overcome evil, how to repair the damage of personal wrongdoing, and how to reach a condition of eternal bliss."[1] To the extent that the Bible plausibly provides such guidance and instruction, its content could itself be at least *some* evidence for the proposition that *a loving God exists who has provided a revelation*.[2]

---

1. Menssen and Sullivan, *Agnostic Inquirer*, 15.
2. This point is argued at length in Menssen and Sullivan, *Agnostic Inquirer*, see especially 62–119.

The Bible Itself as Evidence?

But is the content of the Bible just the sort of message we would expect a loving God to convey to his creatures? Many would answer that it is not. Even many believers find many biblical passages disturbing from a moral point of view or otherwise unhelpful. So, a "yes" answer here is by no means obviously correct.

I will discuss morally disturbing examples momentarily but here are some examples of "otherwise unhelpful" content in the Bible. Even many believers find large parts of Leviticus, Numbers, and Deuteronomy dull and uninspiring. And many people find the various genealogies in the Bible to be soporific. Moreover, even the great books of prophecy, such as Isaiah, Jeremiah, and Ezekiel, contain numerous passages that seem obscure, bewildering, and/or uninteresting to many (perhaps most) readers. For virtually everyone, the first nine chapters of 1 Chronicles (and many other chapters of that book) are tedious in the extreme—essentially just a long list of names. And how many Christians find the book of Nehemiah helpful in their spiritual lives? I suspect very few. The book of Ecclesiastes presents readers with an entirely different sort of challenge, for it articulates a profoundly pessimistic view of human life—"vanity of vanities! All is vanity" (1:2 NRSV)—albeit with a seemingly "tacked on" pious conclusion (12:13–14). In fact, as is well-known, many Christians do little Bible reading, and they find reading much of it unrewarding. Is a book with all these features *just the sort of communication we would expect* from an almighty, loving God? I think many would answer "no."

5

Obstacles (Old Testament)

SUPPOSE WE KNOW OR reasonably believe that an almighty, loving God exists. What obstacles stand in the way of showing that the Bible is the word of God? In this chapter I will focus on obstacles arising from the content of the Old Testament. But let me start by noting three general philosophical obstacles.

First, we don't know for sure who wrote many of the books of the Bible. Even theologically conservative scholars admit that this is so. Second, even if we know who wrote a given book, how could we know whether God guided the author's thoughts? We cannot look into the human author's mind and locate divine activity there. Third, which books are under consideration? For example, are we talking about the Hebrew Bible or the Christian Bible? And what about other sacred books, such as the Qur'an or the Hindu scriptures? Can they be divinely inspired too, or are they ruled out for some reason?

Beyond these general philosophical obstacles, the content of the Bible raises hard questions from various points of view—moral, theological, historical, and scientific. Many passages in the

Obstacles (Old Testament)

Bible involve claims that are very implausible, morally troubling, or theologically disconcerting for thoughtful readers. Such passages can be used to argue that the Bible is not (or cannot possibly be) a message from a God of love. Here is a partial list of problematic passages in the Old Testament:

- Genesis 1. The author of Gen 1 apparently means to say that God created fruit trees (and other vegetation) *before* creating the sun. Plants, including fruit trees, are created on day *three* of creation while the sun, moon, and stars are created on day *four*—Gen 1:11, 16. But according to contemporary science, the earth orbited the sun for roughly a billion years before there was any life on earth. (According to contemporary science, the sun and the earth are about 4.5 billion years old; the earliest life on earth appeared about 3.5 billion years ago.)

  Note: admittedly, the problems of "creation chronology" in Gen 1 and 2 can be avoided if the texts are interpreted as a kind of theological poetry, in which the author is understood to be making no claims about the temporal sequence of the creation events. Rather, the author is making theological claims in a dramatic, figurative fashion—claims such as: (a) God created all of physical reality, (b) what God created is good, and (c) the Creator should be worshiped, not the things created. Since, however, many Christians reject such figurative interpretations of Gen 1 and 2, they must face questions regarding the chronology of creation.

- Genesis 1 and 2. In Gen 1 plants are created on the third day, birds and fish on the fifth day, and land animals in general—followed by humans—on the sixth day. So, the author of Gen 1 apparently indicates that God created human beings, both male and female, *after* creating the plants and animals (Gen 1:11–27). But the author of Gen 2 apparently asserts that God created a male human *before* creating the plants and animals: "In the day the Lord God made the earth and the heavens, when no plant of the field was yet in the earth and no herb of the field had yet sprung up—[. . .] then the Lord God formed man from the dust of the ground, and breathed into his nostrils the breath of life; and the man became a living being" (Gen 2:4–7 NRSV). And in Gen 2, the animals were then created as helpers for the man: "Then the Lord God said, 'It is not good that the man should be alone; I will make him a helper as his partner.' So out of the ground the Lord God formed every animal of the field and every bird of the air, and brought them to the man . . ." (Gen 2: 18–19 NRSV). But the animals didn't turn out to be helpers, so God created a woman (Gen 2:20–22). The point is that the sequence of creation given in Gen 2 conflicts logically with the sequence given in Gen 1. And if that's right, then both accounts cannot be true.[1]

- Genesis 5. Here we have a famous genealogy that provides remarkable ages for various men. For example, Adam lived for 930 years (5:5), Seth lived for 912 years (5:8), and Methuselah lived to be 969 years old (5:27). And interestingly, "After Noah was five hundred years old, Noah became the father of Shem, Ham, and Japeth" (5:32 NRSV). Of course, these ages would seem to be impossible, given what we know about human biology.

- Genesis 6–7. The human beings God created sin a lot, so God drowns all but eight of them in a huge flood. Did God know prior to creating humans that the result would be a world containing almost exclusively wicked people that he would destroy in a flood? Why then create such humans? Or was the almighty, all-knowing, and loving Creator surprised at human sin and without a better means of dealing with it? Was a

---

1. The NIV translates Gen 2:19 as follows: "Now the Lord God *had* formed out of the ground all the wild animals and all the birds in the sky" (italics added). This would seem to allow that God created the animals at some earlier time *before* he created a human being. But scholarly translations do not commonly include the word "had" here, among them RSV (Revised Standard Version), OJB (Orthodox Jewish Bible), YLT (Young's Literal Translation), KJV (King James Version), NKJV (New King James Version), RSVCE (Revised Standard Version Catholic Edition), ASV (American Standard Version), and CJB (Complete Jewish Bible). So, the NIV translation is questionable, especially in the context of verses 4–7.

terrifying method of mass extermination the only or best way to deal with the problem of wickedness?

- Genesis 22. God commands a loyal follower (Abraham) to kill his son (Isaac) and burn him on an altar. This famous episode raises a host of questions. Is the command to kill Isaac what we would expect from a God of love? Is human sacrifice morally wrong? (How would you view a contemporary who claimed that God commanded him to kill his son or daughter?) The author of Hebrews says that Abraham "reasoned that God could even raise the dead"—11:19 (NIV). From this perspective, if Abraham kills Issac, Isaac's death isn't necessarily permanent. But wouldn't stabbing one's son to death still be profoundly traumatic for both the son and the father? And is putting a human creature through so extreme a test an act of love? Finally, if God once commanded a father to kill his son, why suppose God would not issue a similar command to other parents, even today? What sort of God is Yahweh?

- Exodus 22:18 (NIV). "Do not allow a sorceress to live." This is just one of *many* passages in which punishments—supposedly approved by God—seem unduly harsh and unjust. (More to follow.) No reputable Christian ethicist would endorse such punishments today.

At this juncture, two comments regarding divine justice may be helpful. (1) *All sins are equal* is a popular claim in some Christian circles. And if all sins are equal, then presumably they all deserve the same punishment—and why not the death penalty? But *all sins are equal* is not only contrary to common sense; it is contradicted by Christ himself, who says to Pilate, "You would have no power over me if it were not given to you from above. Therefore the one who handed me over to you is guilty of a *greater sin*"—John 19:11 (NIV), italics added. Furthermore, 1 John 5:16–17 makes a distinction between mortal sins and non-mortal sins. And the following verse surely implies that some sins are worse than others: they [the scribes] "devour widows' houses and for the sake of appearance say long prayers. They will receive the *greater condemnation*"—Mark 12:40 (NRSV), italics added.

(2) In Christian theology, God's goodness is typically characterized in terms of both love and justice. But Christian theologians have disagreed about the relation between love and justice, especially about the nature of justice. Some deny that there is any tension between God's love and God's justice. God does not suffer from any internal motivational conflicts. Others hold that divine love can conflict with divine justice. The conflict can take two forms. Some hold that one cannot act out of love and out of justice simultaneously; the one motivation excludes the other. And some even allow that on occasion, divine justice calls for actions that are contrary to love. Since the relation between divine love and justice is controversial, I think it best to delay a discussion of it.[2] In the meantime, I hope that any claims I make about justice will seem intuitively correct (or at least plausible) to most readers.

- Exodus 31:15 (ESV). "Whoever does any work on the Sabbath day shall be put to death." Does the punishment fit the "crime"? Would we expect a God of love and justice to demand such a punishment?

- Exodus 34:7 (NIV). The Lord "does not leave the guilty unpunished; he punishes the children and their children *for the sin of the parents* to the third and fourth generation" (italics added). (This declaration is repeated in Num 14:18.) Is punishing a person's children, grandchildren, and great-grandchildren activity we would expect from a God of justice? Indeed, aren't these verses contradicted by other Old Testament passages? For example, "The one who sins is the one who will die. The child will not share the guilt of the parent, nor will the parent share the guilt of the child. The righteousness of the righteous will be credited to them, and the wickedness of the wicked will be charged against them" (Ezek 18:20 NIV). Similarly, "Parents shall not be put to death for

---

2. For an insightful, sustained discussion of the relation between divine love and justice, see Wolterstorff, *Justice in Love*.

Obstacles (Old Testament)

their children, nor shall children be put to death for their parents; only for their own crimes may persons be put to death" (Deut 24:16 NRSV).

- Leviticus 4 (and *many* other passages). God requires that animals be sacrificed to atone for the sins of humans. For example, "If anyone of the common people sins unintentionally in doing any one of the things that by the Lord's commandments ought not to be done, and realizes his guilt, . . . he shall bring for his offering a goat, a female without blemish, for his sin which he has committed. And he shall lay his hand on the head of the sin offering and kill the sin offering . . ." (Lev 4:27–29 ESV).[3] What is puzzling here is why a God of love would want animals killed in this way.

A note about animal sacrifice may be needed here. Some people assume that the animals were *punished* for the sins of humans, so the humans wouldn't have to be punished. But the Bible does not say this. Moreover, what sense would that make? We cannot satisfy the demands of justice by punishing the innocent. (If Joe deserves the death penalty for murder, can justice be satisfied by putting his innocent sister to death?) From a Christian point of view, the animal sacrifices of the Old Testament are all the more puzzling given New Testament teaching, specifically, "It is impossible for the blood of bulls and goats to take away sins" (Heb 10:4 NIV). Of course, the book of Hebrews also says that the Old Testament law is "a shadow of the good things to come" (10:1 ESV). Thus, some claim that the animal sacrifices were a necessary preparation for understanding Christ's sacrifice. But how plausible is that? Within modern secular cultures there is no practice of animal sacrifice. And both "Jainism and Buddhism rejected the sacrificial system . . . taught in the Vedas."[4] Are people in cultures such as these, without a practice of animal sacrifice, unable to understand and accept the gospel? Surely not.

---

3. For more about animal sacrifice in the Old Testament, see Lev 1–4, 12, 16; Exod 29; Num 28.

4. Hopfe, *Religions of the World*, 98.

Is the Bible the Word of God?

- Leviticus 20:9 (NRSV). "All who curse father or mother shall be put to death." Is this punishment consistent with the lex talionis—the "eye for an eye" principle (Lev 24:19–20)? Is so harsh a punishment proportional to the offense? Is it what we would expect from a God of justice?

- Leviticus 20:10 (NIV). "If a man commits adultery with another man's wife—with the wife of his neighbor—both the adulterer and the adulteress must be put to death." Adultery is wrong, of course, but is the death penalty commensurate with the offense?

- Leviticus 20:13 (NRSV). "If a man lies with a male as with a woman, both of them have committed an abomination; they shall be put to death; their blood is upon them." Even if one thinks that homosexual acts are immoral, the question remains: is the death penalty proportional to the alleged offense?

- Leviticus 21:9 (NRSV). "When the daughter of a priest profanes herself through prostitution, she profanes her father; *she shall be burned to death*" (italics added). Is the punishment here not only disproportionate to the offense but also "cruel and unusual"? Would a God of love and justice demand such punishment?

- Numbers 12:1–16. In this passage Moses's sister and brother, Miriam and Aaron, criticize him "because of the Cushite woman whom he had married . . ." (12:1 ESV). This criticizing angered the Lord (v. 9), so the Lord gave Miriam leprosy—she became "leprous, like snow" (12:10 ESV). Isn't this action of God's rather shocking? A little beyond the bounds of "tough love"? Later in the passage, in response to Moses's prayer, God removes the leprosy. But still, are God's actions in this passage just what we would expect if God is loving?

- Deuteronomy 20:16–18 (NIV). "However, in the cities of the nations the Lord your God is giving you as an inheritance, do not leave alive anything that breathes. Completely destroy them—the Hittites, Amorites, Canaanites, Perizzites,

Obstacles (Old Testament)

Hivites and Jebusites—*as the Lord your God has commanded you*. Otherwise, they will teach you to follow all the detestable things they do in worshiping their gods, and you will sin against the LORD your God" (italics added). These verses represent God as commanding the Israelites to commit genocide or at least mass slaughter. Is that what we should expect from a God of love? If one group of people will tempt another group to sin, does that justify killing the tempters?

- Joshua 6:21 (NIV). "They devoted the city to the LORD and destroyed with the sword every living thing in it—*men and women, young and old, cattle, sheep and donkeys*" (italics added). In a similar vein, consider "when Israel had finished killing all the men of Ai in the fields and in the desert where they had chased them, and when every one of them had been put to the sword, all the Israelites returned to Ai and killed those who were in it. *Twelve thousand men and women fell that day*—all the people of Ai" (Josh 8:24–25 NIV, italics added). Also, consider: "And the LORD gave them [i.e., a large army combined of Amorites, Hittites, Perizzites, etc.] into the hand of Israel. They defeated them and pursued them all the way to Greater Sidon, to Misrephoth Maim, and to the Valley of Mizpah on the east, until no survivors were left. Joshua did to them as the Lord had directed; he hamstrung their horses and burned their chariots" (Josh 11:8–9 NIV).

The actions described in these verses were taken in response to divine commands, according to the biblical text. Note that not only combatants, but women, children, and even animals were killed in some cases. (Hamstringing the horses would leave them unable to walk.) Would we expect a God of love to demand such mass killings?

Note: It has been argued that the descriptions of mass killings in the Old Testament are hyperbolic, merely conventional Ancient Near Eastern ways of claiming victory in warfare, not to be taken literally. As an analogy, think of how a basketball player, if asked how the game went, might respond "we slaughtered them."[5] But as far as I can see, the descriptions in these verses (and some others) are not plausibly interpreted as deliberate exaggerations. They are too detailed and specific for that.

- Joshua 10:40 (NIV). "So Joshua subdued the whole region, including the hill country, the Negev, the western foothills and the mountain slopes, together with all their kings. He left no survivors. *He totally destroyed all who breathed, just as the Lord, the God of Israel, had commanded*" (italics added). This verse surely seems to be saying that God commanded genocide. Would a God of love do that?

Note: while the book of Joshua describes a dramatic military conquest of Canaan by the Israelites, many Bible scholars and archeologists claim that the account in Joshua is inaccurate or at least greatly exaggerated. As Professor Rodney Stark observes, "The best of the archeologically informed historians now believe that the Jews did not conquer Israel after their long stay in the wilderness, but settled peacefully."[6] For present purposes, however, there are at least two issues to bear in mind here: (1) Whether or not the Israelites committed genocide, the book of Joshua apparently represents God as approving genocide. (2) If the account in Joshua is historically inaccurate, can it still be a message from God?

- First Samuel 15:2–3 (NRSV). Samuel said to Saul, "Thus says the Lord of hosts, 'I will punish the Amalekites for what they did in opposing the Israelites when they came up out of Egypt. Now go and attack Amalek, and utterly destroy all that they have; *do not spare them; but kill both man and woman, child and infant, ox and sheep, camel and donkey*'" (italics added). Would we expect a God of love and justice to command the killing even of innocents, such as children, infants, and animals?

---

5. See Copan, *Is God a Moral Monster?* 170–75.
6. Stark, *Discovering God*, 171.

Obstacles (Old Testament)

- Second Samuel 6:6–7 (ESV). "And when they came to the threshing floor of Nacon, Uzzah put out his hand to the ark of God and took hold of it, for the oxen stumbled. And the anger of the Lord was kindled against Uzzah, and God struck him down there because of his error, and he died there beside the ark of God." (This story is repeated in 1 Chr 13:9–10.) Now, it's true that the men transporting the ark did not follow the instructions for moving it. The men were supposed to carry the ark on their shoulders, not transport it on a cart (Num 4:5–6; 7:9). Still, does moving the ark in a different way merit death? Is killing Uzzah how most people would expect a God of love to react in such a case?

- Second Kings 2:23–24 (ESV). In this passage, forty-two youths jeer at the prophet Elisha, "Go up, you baldhead!" (These words are perhaps roughly equivalent to "get lost, you old codger."[7]) Elisha curses the youths, and two bears maul them, apparently as divine retribution. Now, the disrespect of the youths is manifest, but still, would most people expect a just and loving God to have them slain by bears?

- Psalm 6:5 (NIV). "No one remembers you [the Lord] when he is dead. Who praises you from the grave?" Consider also "to you, Lord, I called; to the Lord I cried for mercy: 'What gain is there in my destruction, in my going down into the pit? Will the dust praise you? Will it proclaim your faithfulness?'" (Ps 30:8–9 NIV). And "Do you show your wonders to the dead? Do those who are dead rise up and praise you? Is your love declared in the grave . . . ?" (Ps 88:10–11 NIV). In context all these rhetorical questions are plainly to be answered in the negative. Thus, these psalms, in line with nearly all the Old Testament books, show no knowledge of a blessed life with God after death. Would you expect a God of love to leave believers ignorant of heaven and hell, if such are realities? (While the book of Daniel, one of last books written in the Old Testament, does mention a resurrection of the dead—see

---

7. See Kaiser et al., *Hard Sayings*, 233.

Dan 12:2—there is no indication that the Patriarchs, Moses, the judges, the kings, or even prophets such as Isaiah, Jeremiah, Obadiah, and Amos knew of a blessed life with God after death.)

- Psalm 137:9 (ESV). "Blessed shall he be who takes your little ones and dashes them against the rock!" The psalmist is speaking here of revenge against the Babylonians. Are we to assume that God approves of killing Babylonian babies?

To sum up, the Old Testament contains many morally or theologically disturbing passages. Most importantly, it often represents God as commanding, doing, or approving something that most people would not expect a God of love and justice to command, do, or approve.

6

Obstacles (New Testament)

I'VE BEEN ASKING THIS question: "Is some of the content of the Bible an obstacle to showing that the Bible is the word of God?" In this chapter I focus on obstacles arising from the content of the New Testament.

- Matthew 25:41, 46 (NRSV). "Then he will say to those at his left hand, 'You that are accursed, depart from me into the eternal fire prepared for the devil and his angels'; [. . .] And these will go away into eternal punishment, but the righteous into eternal life." Given that no human can inflict eternal suffering on another, does literally *eternal* punishment fit any offense humans can commit? Does it conform even to so harsh a principle as the lex talionis (an "eye for an eye")? Furthermore, is inflicting eternal suffering plausibly consistent with loving the damned? Why not annihilate them instead (assuming they can't be reformed)?
- Matthew 26:24 (NIV). ". . . woe to that man who betrays the Son of Man! It would be better for him if he had not been born." If we put this verse together with one in the Gospel

of John, hard questions arise: "For Jesus had known from the beginning . . . who would betray him" (John 6:64 NIV). Of course, it was Judas Iscariot who betrayed Jesus ("the Son of Man"). If Jesus knew *from the beginning* that Judas would betray him, why would he select Judas as one of the twelve apostles (Luke 6:13–16)? Moreover, if we make the traditional assumption that an omniscient God knew before creating Judas that "it would be better for him if he had not been born," why would God create Judas?[1] How is it an act of love for God to create someone if he knows it would be better for that person not to be born?

- Mark 7:9–10 (NIV). "Then he [Jesus] said to them 'You have a fine way of setting aside the commands of God in order to observe your own traditions! For Moses said, *Honor your father and your mother*, and, *Anyone who curses his father or mother must be put to death*.'" Is Jesus here endorsing the teaching of Lev 20:9?

- Mark 13:30 (ESV). "Truly I say to you, this generation will not pass away until all these things take place." What are "these things"? In context, they seem to include "the sun will be darkened, and the moon will not give its light, and the stars will be falling from heaven, and the powers in the heavens will be shaken. And then they will see the Son of Man coming in clouds with great power and glory. And then he will send out the angels and gather his elect from the four winds, from the ends of the earth to the ends of heaven" (24–27 ESV). This passage has been deeply puzzling to many because it seems to represent Jesus as predicting that his second coming will happen during the *lifetime of his audience*—presumably sometime in the mid-to-late first century CE. Would we expect God to provide a false—or at least a misleading—prediction about something so important?

---

1. For challenges to the traditional assumption that God has complete or exhaustive foreknowledge, see Boyd, "Open Theism View," 13–54 and Layman, *God*, 151–85.

Obstacles (New Testament)

- John 14:13–14 (ESV). "Whatever you ask in my name, this I will do, that the Father may be glorified in the Son. If you ask me anything in my name, I will do it." Has this promise been kept? How many Christians have prayed for, say, the healing of a loved one, only to find that God has not provided what they asked for? Would we expect a God of love to keep his promises?

- Ephesians 6:5 (NRSV). "Slaves, obey your earthly masters with fear and trembling, in singleness of heart, as you obey Christ." (Similar commands appear in Col 3:22–24, 1 Tim 6:1–2, and Titus 2:9–10.) Contemporary Christian ethicists insist that slavery is wrong, but historically, passages such as Eph 6:5 have been used by many Christians to justify slavery. And isn't such a use of these passages entirely predictable?

- First Timothy 2:11–14 (NIV). "A woman should learn in quietness and full submission. I do not permit a woman to teach or to have authority over a man; she must be silent. For Adam was formed first, then Eve. And Adam was not the one deceived; it was the woman who was deceived and became a sinner." In many Christian denominations, these verses have been (and still are) used to deny women top leadership roles. Does God think women are not capable of top leadership roles, such as priest, pastor, or bishop? Or what?

- Revelation 14: 9–11 (NRSV). "Then another angel, a third, followed them, crying with a loud voice, 'Those who worship the beast and its image . . . will also drink the wine of God's wrath . . . and they will be tormented with fire and sulfur in the presence of the holy angels and in the presence of the Lamb. *And the smoke of their torment goes up for ever and ever.* There is no rest day or night for those who worship the beast and its image and for anyone who receives the mark of its name'" (italics added). Once again, is literally everlasting suffering a proportionate punishment for any human offense? Also, if we assume, as many theologians do, that God knows (in detail) what people would do, if created, then he creates some people knowing they will go to hell; in that case, is creating them an act of love?

- Revelation 1:1 (NIV). "The revelation of Jesus Christ which God gave him to show his servants what must soon take place." Indeed, "the time is near" (1:3 NIV). And consider these additional quotations from the book of Revelation: "The Lord . . . sent his angel to show his servants the things that must soon take place" (22:6 NIV); "Do not seal up the words of the prophecy of this book, because the time is near" (22:10); "Behold I [the Lord Jesus] am coming soon!" (22:12 NIV); and "He who testifies to these things says, "Yes, I am coming soon" (22:20 NIV). While "soon" is a vague word, is it plausible to think the human author of these verses had over two thousand years in mind? Or that his intended audience would assume that "soon" allows for two or more millennia? (I've heard it suggested that since "a thousand years is as a day" to the Lord, "soon" could allow for extremely long periods of time by earthly, human standards. But this approach empties the word "soon" of meaning; for example, by this logic, we could simply rewrite Rev 22:12 along these lines: "Behold, I am coming sometime or other.")

The list of problematic Bible passages (in this chapter and the previous one) is not intended to be complete; merely illustrative. And remember, the crucial question is whether the above passages express just the sort of message *we would expect* a loving God to convey to his creatures? Even many believers would, in honesty, answer "no" to that question.

There are whole books devoted to trying to explain how these puzzling passages fit in with the claim that a just and loving God exists.[2] The need for explanation itself underscores the problem. On the face of it, the content of these passages is not what we would expect as a message from a God of love.

---

2. For example, Kaiser et al., *Hard Sayings*, and Copan, *Is God a Moral Monster?*

7

Curley's Illuminating Reductio

THE DIFFICULTY POSED BY problem passages in the Bible can be clarified by considering an illuminating reductio ad absurdum (reduction to absurdity) argument formulated by the philosopher Edwin Curley. Curley's argument focuses on *morally* problematic passages. It begins with the following three premises:

1. God is a supremely perfect being, who possesses all perfections, including moral perfection.
2. The Bible is the inspired word of God.
3. In many places the Bible represents God as authorizing—that is, either commanding or giving permission for—conduct which is clearly morally wrong.[1]

Christian theologians in general accept premises 1 and 2. And many items on the list of problematic Bible passages provided in chapter five apparently support 3. Most people would agree that genocide is wrong, that child sacrifice is wrong, that it's wrong

---

1. Curley, "Reply to Van Inwagen," 85.

Is the Bible the Word of God?

to administer the death penalty to a son for cursing his parents, wrong to administer the death penalty for adultery, wrong to burn a prostitute to death (if her father is a priest), and so on. Therefore, 3 is hard to deny.

But if premises 1 and 2 are true, it would seem to follow that:

> 4. The Bible does not seriously misrepresent God's moral nature by repeatedly portraying him as authorizing conduct he did not authorize.[2]

But don't statements 3 and 4 together imply:

> 5. God did repeatedly authorize conduct which was clearly morally wrong?[3]

And yet, premise 1 surely implies that:

> 6. God would never authorize conduct which is clearly morally wrong.[4]

Since statements 5 and 6 are logically inconsistent, it appears that we must give up one of the premises that give rise to the inconsistency, that is, we must give up at least one of premises 1, 2, and 3—or else we must reject one of the inferences made in arriving at statements 5 and 6.

Where does Curley's reasoning go wrong if it does go wrong? Curley himself thinks that premise 2 needs to go—the Bible is not the word of God, it is not divinely inspired, and it is not a reliable authority on moral issues. The Bible is a merely human book.

Some Christian thinkers, commonly regarded as "liberal," such as Albert Schweitzer and Harry Emerson Fosdick, agree with Curley. The Bible is not divinely inspired, not divinely revealed, and not the word of God.

Neo-orthodox theologians such as Karl Barth and Emil Brunner agree that the Bible is not a revelation—rather, Jesus Christ himself is the revelation. The Bible is a record of that revelation

---

2. Curley, "Reply to Van Inwagen," 86.
3. Curley, "Reply to Van Inwagen," 86.
4. Curley, "Reply to Van Inwagen," 86.

insofar as it tells us how Jesus lived and taught. It is intended to lead us to a personal encounter with Christ. It is not intended to reveal a set of propositions (or statements) for us to believe. Hence, any factual or moral errors in the Bible are not a problem; we are not meant to glean propositional truth from it, as if it were a theological textbook. *Revelation is personal encounter with God and Christ*; it is not propositional in nature.

More traditional Christian thinkers typically deny the third premise of Curley's reductio: "In many places the Bible represents God as authorizing—that is, either commanding or giving permission for—conduct which is clearly morally wrong." For example, many Christian thinkers maintain that the Bible is a revelation and, indeed, it is an infallible guide to propositional truth *when correctly interpreted*. Of course, there are many incorrect interpretations of the Bible—Christian thinkers in general agree about that. But the Bible, properly interpreted, contains no falsehoods whatsoever. (This claim applies to the original manuscripts or autographs; some minor errors may have been introduced as manuscripts were copied down through history.) Let us refer to this view as *Infallibilism*.

Finally, some Christian theologians claim that the Bible reveals truths (propositions), *and only truths*, as regards matters of faith—theology and morality, but it does contain some errors on historical and scientific matters. These errors can be identified through the usual methods of historians and scientists. Let us refer to this view as *Neo-traditionalism*.

I myself reject all of these responses to Curley's reductio. Later on, I will propose an alternative response to it, and I will also argue that the Bible is a divinely authorized source of truth, though it is by no means infallible—not even on theological and moral matters. (Keep in mind that we humans constantly make use of fallible authorities in our daily lives—encyclopedias, medical doctors, maps, news reporters, textbooks, and so on.) But for now, let's examine attempts to defend Infallibilism and Neo-traditionalism. Adherents of these views deny that the Bible *ever* represents God as authorizing conduct which is morally wrong.

8

A Popular Solution Fails

SOME BELIEVERS TRY TO deal with the morally problematic passages listed above (in chapters 5 and 6) by claiming that "whatever an almighty being does or commands (or approves) is right." This popular solution won't work, for multiple reasons.

First, might does not make right, according to Judeo-Christian morality. So, the claim that *whatever an almighty being does or commands (or approves) is right* makes no sense in terms of the morality believers themselves endorse.

Second, it simply isn't plausible to suggest that whatever an almighty being does or commands is right. Would child abuse in general be right if God commanded it? Torturing the innocent? Blinding people? Kidnapping? Racism? Rape? How about breaking a promise? If God promises that people can be saved by faith and then breaks that promise, is breaking the promise morally permissible because an almighty being can do no wrong? A "yes" answer to these questions is simply not plausible.

If the reply is that God would not command (do or approve) any of these things, the reply misses the point entirely. For on this

A Popular Solution Fails

view, *there is no moral standard independent of God's will*. Hence, nothing an almighty being commands (does or approves) is wrong, according to this view. In addition, many of the problem passages are problematic precisely because they represent God as commanding, doing, or approving something morally shocking, such as genocide, burning prostitutes to death, or punishing children for the sins of their parents.

Third, consider this question: "what are some things that a thoroughly evil, almighty being would do or command?" Punish the innocent? Reward the wicked? Prevent human happiness in general? Inflict pain on helpless creatures? Damn those who die as infants to eternal hell? But if whatever an almighty being does or commands (or approves) is right, then all of these things would be right if done or commanded by an almighty God. By this logic, then, God can do or command anything a thoroughly evil deity would do or command and *still count as good and still be worthy of worship*. So, in this approach, the content of "good"—as in "God is good"—has been emptied of significant meaning.

Some may reply, "But God isn't merely almighty. God is loving and just." Now, however, we have the problem of a supposedly loving and just God doing or commanding or approving things that seem *plainly* unloving and/or unjust. And this just isn't plausible.

Here it should be noted that Christian thinkers have taken various positions on the relation between God and ethics, including the following:

- *Theological voluntarists* hold (roughly) that God's will is the ultimate standard in ethics and there is no limit on what God can will. Thus, if God were to command "hate thy neighbor," hating one's neighbor would be a duty.

- *Divine command theorists* hold that an act is a duty if (and because) a *loving* God commands it, and an act is wrong if (and because) a *loving* God forbids it. On this view, there are many things a loving God would not command and *could* not command while remaining a God of love.

- *Natural law theorists* hold that morality is grounded in our God-given nature as human beings. True moral laws promote human fulfillment or flourishing. Natural law theorists typically emphasize that we should obey God's commands because God, our Creator, knows what is best for us.[1]
- *Agapism*—at a first approximation—is the view that "love your neighbor as yourself" is the fundamental rule of ethics. (*Agape* is one of the Greek words for love which appears in the New Testament.) On this view, love involves caring about one's neighbor as one cares about oneself. (A person may not feel affection for himself but may still take care of himself by eating a healthy diet, exercising regularly, and so on.) Versions of agapism differ in regard to (a) what caring involves and (b) who one's neighbor is.[2]

Here is one last point to keep in mind. As we've already seen, not all of the problematic biblical passages concern what God does or commands or approves. Some appear to be factual errors, such as the claim that fruit trees existed before the sun (Gen 1:11, 16), that a human being existed before there were any plants and animals (Gen 2:5–7, 18–19), that Methuselah lived to be 969 years old (Gen 5:27), and that the second coming of Christ would happen soon (or shortly) after the book of Revelation was written (Rev 1:1 and 22:7). These problems are left untouched by the claim that whatever an almighty being does or commands (or approves) is

---

1. For a defense of theological voluntarism, see Henry, "Good as the Will of God." For more about the divine command theory, see Adams, *Finite and Infinite Goods* (especially chapters 1 and 10–12). For a statement of the natural law view, see Boyd and VanArragon, "Ethics Is Based on Natural Law." The alternatives to theological voluntarism must deny that God can will just anything or that God can will just anything and remain good. Often the claim is that certain ethical truths, such as "love is good," are *necessary truths*. A necessary truth is one that cannot be false under any circumstances.

2. The best current statement of agapism is undoubtedly in Wolterstorff, *Justice in Love* (see esp. 21–157). Wolterstorff stresses that agape love involves caring about a person's well-being but also caring about whether she is treated in accord with her worth (i.e., with respect). Furthermore, in seeking the well-being of oneself or others, one must never wrong anyone.

A Popular Solution Fails

right. And so, they remain as problems for Infallibilism. Since the second coming is a theological matter, the last item on the list also raises a question about Neo-traditionalism.

9

God's Thoughts Are Higher Than Ours

FACED WITH PROBLEMATIC MORAL passages in the Bible, many believers appeal to Isaiah 55:8–9 (NIV): "'For my thoughts are not your thoughts, neither are your ways my ways,' declares the LORD. 'As the heavens are higher than the earth, so are my ways higher than your ways and my thoughts than your thoughts.'" In short, we are in no position to make claims about what God would or wouldn't do. What may seem unloving to us may be loving in some way we simply cannot see. God always knows better than we (humans) do.

There are several problems with an appeal to the Isaiah passage as a response to the philosophical problem at issue. First, the passage is taken out of context. In context, Isa 55:8–9 indicates God's willingness to forgive the wicked—which may come as a surprise, especially to people convinced of their own righteousness. "Let the wicked forsake his way and the evil man his thoughts. Let him turn to the LORD, and he will have mercy on him, and to our God, for he will freely pardon" (Isa 55:7 NIV). *Taken in context, verses 8–9 are about God's surprising willingness to forgive the wicked (who repent), they are not about a way of handling theological and philosophical problems in general.* Unfortunately, Christians often use these verses as a way of dodging hard questions. Simply put, the verses are often quoted as a way of "copping out."

Second, keep in mind the philosophical context. The appeal to Isa 55:8–9 is a way of saying *we have no idea what to expect from a loving God*—"God's ways are not our ways." In context then, the appeal to Isa 55:8–9 undermines any attempt to claim that the content of the Bible conveys a message *we would expect* from a God of love. From this perspective, we simply don't know what to expect! We're clueless.

Third, as applied in the present philosophical context, the appeal to Isa 55:8–9 empties "God is good" of significant meaning. God might command child abuse. Or torturing the innocent. God might send newborn infants to hell. "God's ways are not our ways." Who are we to say what God would or wouldn't do? By this logic, a good God could do anything an evil deity might do. Thus, a common misapplication of Isa 55:8–9 empties "God is good" of significant meaning.

Fourth, why limit "God's thoughts are higher" to a defense of problematic *biblical* texts? For example, why not use it to defend multiple revelations? Perhaps God has authorized not only the Bible but also the Talmud, the Qur'an, the Upanishads, the Avesta, the Tripitaka, and the Book of Mormon. Why not? If you think this would be a misapplication of "God's thoughts are higher," on what principle do you limit its application? Because only the Bible is divinely inspired? In context, of course, this would beg the question (assume the point to be proved).

Finally, bear in mind that the "God's thoughts are higher" move does not solve the problem of apparent factual errors, such as the claim that fruit trees existed before the sun did (Gen 1:11, 16), that Noah lived to be 950 years old (Gen 9:29), and that Jesus' second coming occurred before Jesus' generation passed away (Mark 13:30). As noted previously, these problems remain for Infallibilism, and the last item, concerning Jesus' second coming, raises a question the Neo-traditionalist must address.

10

Killing and Moral Theology

HERE IS ANOTHER ATTEMPTED solution for biblical passages that are morally troubling—in particular, a proposed solution for passages in which God commands genocide (or mass killing), child sacrifice (e.g., the Abraham and Isaac story), animal sacrifice, and the death penalty for lesser offenses than murder.

As Creator, God gives life, but he also has the right to take life. (After all, we all die, so death is part of the Creator's grand design.) And if God has the right to take life, then God has the right to appoint humans to take life. God can delegate. Hence, God can command genocide, child sacrifice, animal sacrifice, as well as the death penalty for various wrong acts.

This "solution" is problematic for several reasons. First, God's having the right to take life *does not guarantee that the command to commit genocide (or mass killing) is an act we would expect from a loving God.* In fact, even many believers are greatly troubled by such a command. It doesn't plausibly fit with the claim that God is a God of love. The same goes for commanding Abraham to sacrifice Isaac. And for commanding the mass slaughter of animals (as in 1 Sam 15:3).

Second, God's law is supposed to be just. But many Old Testament passages prescribe unjust punishments. Cursing one's parents is wrong, but it does not merit the death penalty. Such a penalty violates even so stringent a principle as the lex talionis ("an eye for an eye"). A just punishment must be proportional to the crime. Similarly, adultery is wrong, but adulterers do not deserve the death penalty. And would it really be just to burn a woman to death for prostitution if her father is a priest? The answer is surely "no, it would not; it would be terribly cruel and unjust."

Third, it is one thing to have the right to take life, and another to command others to take it. Here's an analogy. Let's assume that parents have the right to punish their children. Can they delegate the punishment to whomever they wish? If spanking is permitted, can parents rightly delegate it to a big brother with plenty of misbehavior to his own credit? To an acquaintance? To a stranger? Shouldn't the punishment come directly from the parents? Granted, an older sibling may be given responsibility for babysitting and with that some very limited right to punish younger siblings (such as "go to the corner"). But what about giving one sinful nation the command to eradicate another sinful nation, to kill even the children? Is that right? If the Creator wants a nation wiped out, he can easily do it himself. Why give sinful people the "go ahead" to commit mass killing? Isn't it a bit like giving a stranger, known for bad behavior himself, permission to physically punish one's children, when one could easily perform the punishment oneself? The point here is that having the right to take life is one thing, delegating the killing to sinful creatures is another.[1]

In this connection we must also consider the psychological effect killing would have on the killers. Killing children and

---

1. Here are some other examples which illustrate that *having a right to do X* does not necessarily carry with it the right to *delegate the doing of X*. Spouses have the right to have sex with one another, but they do not have the right to delegate this activity. And judges have the right to sentence someone found guilty of a crime, but they do not have the right to delegate the sentencing to, say, anyone who happens to visit the courtroom.

pregnant women with a sword, bow, club, or spear would surely have a profound effect on the killers. Perhaps it would make some more callous and brutal. Maybe it would traumatize others. Perhaps others would be plagued with dismaying memories—flashbacks—for the rest of their lives. Could anyone participate in such a slaughter without being profoundly affected? I think we have plenty of evidence from the experience of war that killing often leaves the killer with deep emotional scars.

Fourth, having the right to take life does not necessarily make taking life a loving act. Here's an analogy. Suppose I could donate a kidney to save a stranger who needs a kidney transplant. But the stranger has no right to my kidney, and I have a right to keep it. Suppose I decide to keep my kidney. I do have the right to keep it, in my view, but keeping it is not a loving act. It would not be a wrong act, in my view, but it would not be a loving act. So, even if God has the right to take life, it doesn't follow that we should expect God to command genocide (or mass killing), if God is indeed a God of love.

Fifth, if God commands the Israelites to slaughter the Canaanites, what message does that send to (and about) the Canaanites? Does God love them? The command to kill them all hardly sends a message of love—just the opposite. Furthermore, isn't a strong message of favoritism sent by such a command? God blesses his favorites and has no problem eradicating non-favorites. Simply put, the claim that God is a God of love rings hollow if combined with a divine command to commit genocide.

As regards genocide of the peoples occupying the Holy Land, two specific reasons are often given to justify it. These are taken from the Old Testament itself:

a. Genesis 15:16 (NIV). In this passage God is speaking to Abraham: "In the fourth generation your descendants will come back here, for the sin of the Amorites has not yet reached its full measure."

b. Deuteronomy 20:16–18 (NIV). "However, in the cities of the nations the LORD your God is giving you as an inheritance,

Killing and Moral Theology

do not leave alive anything that breathes. Completely destroy them—the Hittites, Amorites, Canaanites, Perizzites, Hivites and Jebusites—as the LORD your God has commanded you. Otherwise, they will teach you to follow all the detestable things they do in worshiping their gods, and you will sin against the LORD your God."

These passages apparently give two related justifications for genocide. First, the inhabitants of the land were very sinful. Second, if left alive, they would teach the Israelites to sin egregiously.

Should this convince us that the command to kill the inhabitants of the land is what we would expect from a God of love?

In part, these justifications of genocide (or mass killing) raise the same issues we've considered under the "God has the right to take life" justification:

1. God has the right to take life, but what message does the divine command to perform genocide (or mass killing) send to creatures? A message of divine love? Manifestly, it does not. In fact, just the opposite.

2. God has the right to take life, but does that clearly legitimate delegating the killing to sinful human "hit men"? Arguably not, for several reasons. First, what message does such delegating send to humans in general? That God cares about some people or some groups but not others? That God plays favorites? Second, what are the moral effects of mass killing on the killers? Surely killing children and pregnant women would leave moral scars. Third, killing with swords, bows, clubs, and spears undoubtedly inflicts a lot of terror and suffering. Almighty God could painlessly euthanize whole groups—wouldn't that be better? Why doesn't God do that? Finally, as we have already seen, *the right to do X does not necessarily carry with it the right to delegate the doing of X*. For example, having the right to punish one's children does not give one the right to delegate the punishing to strangers when one could easily perform the punishing oneself.

3. Almighty God could easily relocate the Canaanites, so they won't influence the Israelites. Is mass killing a better option than relocation? A more loving option? A "yes" answer is not very plausible.

4. Many people in modern society influence others to sin: to worship "the almighty dollar," to overconsume, to waste their time watching too much TV, to overindulge in video games, to become addicted to gambling or drugs, to hate their political opponents, and so on. Would we be justified in killing these influencers? No, we would not. So, why think killing was justifiable in the case of the Canaanites? (Simply because God said so? That sends us back to chapter eight, "A Popular Solution Fails.")

To sum up, this attempt to show that a God of love might well command genocide (or mass killing) falls well short of the goal.

In closing, let me again note that not all of the morally problematic passages have to do with killing. For example, consider the punishment that God is said to dole out to children and grandchildren for their parents' wrongdoing (Exod 34:7). The punishment need not always be death; it might be some form of suffering or misfortune. It would still be unjust, wouldn't it? And the claim that a woman may not teach or have authority over a man (1 Tim 2:11–14) seems objectionable to many. Finally, what about some of the actions ascribed to God, such as punishing Miriam by infecting her with leprosy (Num 12:1–16)? Or creating a race of humans, *all but eight of whom* were exceedingly wicked (Gen 7–9)—assuming God knew this outcome prior to creation? Or *testing* Abraham by demanding that he sacrifice Isaac (Gen 22)? (Testing Abraham is of course a different act than the act of killing Isaac.) Or creating those destined for eternal hell—assuming God knew, prior to creation, that some were so destined?

To sum up, even if we grant that the Creator has the right to end life, this does not clearly provide a justification for:

a. Delegating mass killing (or genocide) to human beings.

b. Prescribing death as punishment for crimes that do not involve killing (such as adultery).
c. Commanding child sacrifice (as in the case of Abraham and Isaac).
d. Requiring animal sacrifice on a large scale.

We must also keep in mind morally problematic passages that do not involve killing, such as the prohibition on women teaching or having authority over men and the divine punishment of children for the sins of their parents (when the punishment does not involve death). Thus, many biblical passages are morally problematic for both Infallibilism and Neo-traditionalism.

11

Three Approaches to Biblical Interpretation

DIFFERENT APPROACHES TO INTERPRETATION may provide different ways of understanding problematic passages in the Bible. Here I consider three approaches to interpreting the Bible.

One approach to biblical interpretation is very common (and natural) among modern Christians. In this approach, the correct interpretation is whatever the original human author said—be it Moses, Isaiah, Luke, the apostle Paul, and so on. Of course, we can't always be sure of the human author's meaning, but it remains the correct interpretation of the passage in question and the interpretation we rightly seek. And naturally, in order to arrive at the correct interpretation, we need to use the best linguistic, literary, and historical tools available. Let us call this the *Human Author Approach* to biblical interpretation.

Perhaps I should mention that some contemporary scholars reject the Human Author Approach because they think interpreters should focus simply on *the sense of the text*. From this perspective, we need to know nothing about the human author in order to arrive at the best understanding of the text. We simply need to

Three Approaches to Biblical Interpretation

focus on the meaning of the words, sentences, paragraphs, and so on in their wider linguistic context (gospel, epistle, poem, historical work, and so on.)

In practice, I believe the Sense of the Text Approach can *usually* provide the same interpretation as the Human Author Approach. But we do normally make assumptions about the human authors. For example, we assume that the human authors of the Bible do not deliberately contradict themselves. So, if a passage is ambiguous but only one of the meanings is consistent with the rest of the text, we favor that interpretation. Or again, if we judge that a statement in the Bible would have seemed obviously false to the human author if interpreted literally, then we are apt to assume that he used language in a figurative way because we assume he did not intend to assert anything obviously false. And the date of authorship is sometimes relevant to interpreting a text. For example, if 2 Peter was written late in the first century, then it wasn't written by the apostle Peter, and the author is apparently claiming to have witnessed events he didn't witness, such as Christ's transfiguration (2 Pet 1:16–18). And given that the book of Revelation says that the second coming of Jesus will happen "soon" (Rev 1:1), it surely matters whether it was written in 95 CE or 2025 CE.[1]

As far as I can see, in regard to the problems presently at issue, the Sense of the Text Approach yields no advantage over the Human Author Approach. Accordingly, I judge that we can safely set the Sense of the Text Approach aside.

In forming a list of problematic biblical passages, I have to this point employed the Human Author Approach to interpretation. And, as we've seen, many biblical passages seem quite problematic when so interpreted. But for much of Christian history, the Human Author Approach was not the favored approach to biblical

---

1. For a careful examination of what I've called the Sense of the Text Approach, see Wolterstorff, *Divine Discourse*, 130–70. My brief comments here owe a debt to Wolterstorff. It is also worth noting that textual critics make judgments about the motivations of copyists in determining the best version of biblical texts. For example, is a variation in a manuscript merely a mistake (possibly due to inattention), or was it motivated by a theological concern? So, even to settle on the best text, judgments about the motivations of scribes are involved.

interpretation. Leading Christian thinkers such as Irenaeus, Origen, Gregory of Nyssa, and Augustine adopted more complex interpretive approaches. As philosopher Richard Swinburne explains, "Passages in the Old Testament in apparent conflict with the New [Testament] were either to be interpreted as God's temporary and limited revelation superseded by the fuller revelation, or to be interpreted metaphorically."[2] To illustrate, from this perspective, if, say, cursing one's parents is assigned too harsh a punishment in the Old Testament, we could say that the harsh punishment was assigned to communicate to a primitive culture that the act is clearly wrong and deserving of punishment. From the more enlightened perspective of the Christian love ethic, we can see that the act is indeed wrong but not deserving of so harsh a punishment. And the "genocide passages" might be interpreted metaphorically, as not about the literal killing of the Canaanites but about destroying the sinful inclinations and desires typical of the Canaanites (as the ancient Hebrews viewed them).

This more complex approach to biblical interpretation is based, in part, on the insight that the meaning of a text can be altered when its context is altered. To take a modern example (borrowed from Swinburne), towards the end of her career, a scholar might publish a collection of her articles, including articles she thinks contain mistakes, faulty methodology, or fallacious reasoning. She might include a preface explaining the errors in these articles.[3] And she might republish the articles because she thinks they are illustrative of tempting errors, partially correct, or perhaps because they are flawed attempts that *led the way* to something better. Such a preface forces a change in the interpretation of the articles in question. In particular, *the articles must no longer be understood to endorse the specified errors.*

Similarly, by viewing the Bible as a whole, the Old Testament must be interpreted in the context of the New Testament, which supersedes it. And the meaning of many Old Testament passages

---

2. Swinburne, *Revelation*, 257.

3. The example is borrowed in its essentials from Swinburne, "What Does the Old Testament Mean?," 212.

Three Approaches to Biblical Interpretation

may be dramatically changed by this change in context. Let us call this the *Contextual Approach* to biblical interpretation.

Augustine set down a further principle: "Whatever there is in the word of God that cannot, when taken literally, be referred either to purity of life or soundness of doctrine, you may set down as figurative."[4] This underscores the fact that early on in church history, Christian theologians rejected the Human Author Approach to biblical interpretation.

Interestingly, the Contextual Approach may help us understand how divine inspiration or guidance could come at the level of compilation and editing, not only at the stage of initial authorship. The most important cases here would be (a) the selection of the various books (or writings) by the church and (b) the inclusion of the Old Testament in a larger work involving the New Testament. I've just underscored the latter case (b). As for the former case (a), it might *conceivably* be that some documents were not divinely inspired as originally written, say, for example, the book of Ecclesiastes or St. Paul's letter to Philemon. (I am not here denying that these books were written under divine inspiration. I am merely illustrating a possibility.) But if these books were included in the canon of Scripture *under divine guidance*, they would become part of the word of God, having divine authority.

Can the Contextual Approach provide a defense of Infallibilism and/or of Neo-traditionalism? The Contextual Approach allows many problem passages in the Old Testament either to be relegated to the category of superseded revelation or to be interpreted metaphorically. Unlike the Human Author Approach, the Contextual Approach does not necessarily endorse as true what the human authors of the Old Testament said. So, on the Contextual Approach, one might interpret a divine genocidal command figuratively, as the command to conquer evil desires and inclinations. In addition, one might view the practice of animal sacrifices as an accommodation to the beliefs or attitudes of a barbaric culture; the practice is superseded under the new covenant.

---

4. Augustine, *De Doctrina Christiana*, Bk. III, ch. 10, para. 14.

Is the Bible the Word of God?

But does the Contextual Approach really provide an effective explanation of morally problematic passages in the Bible?

First, what does the Contextual Approach imply about the Old Testament *prior* to its being made part of a larger work that includes the New Testament? Consider these examples:

- Was the Old Testament once—before being superseded by the New Testament—correct in assigning the death penalty for cursing one's parents, adultery, Sabbath-breaking, sorcery, and so on? Apparently so. But these punishments seem manifestly disproportionate to the offenses in question and hence unjust. Moreover, the disproportionate nature of these punishments did not change over time.

- Was the Old Testament once—before being superseded by the New Testament—correct in indicating that God punishes children for the sins of their parents? Wouldn't a literal interpretation of passages such as Exod 34:7 have been correct before the New Testament was combined with the Old Testament?

- The Israelites reportedly committed mass slaughter (at least sometimes) in response to a divine command (1 Sam 15). Did such events actually occur? Prior to combining the Old Testament with the New Testament, wouldn't a literal interpretation of these passages have been correct? I assume so. Well, then, was the divinely ordered mass killing morally justified "back in the day"? I think adherents of the Contextual Approach must answer "yes."

- Was the practice of animal sacrifice once right, even though it involved killing many innocent animals (and not because they were needed for food)? But does the practice of animal sacrifice treat animals in accordance with their true value? Many would say it does not. In any case, adherents of the Contextual Approach can hardly claim that the ancient Hebrews did not (literally!) practice animal sacrifice.

Three Approaches to Biblical Interpretation

- Did God literally command Abraham to commit human (child) sacrifice? In the absence of the context provided by the New Testament, the answer would seem to be "yes."

To sum up, even if the Contextual Approach gives Christians some promising resources for interpreting the Old Testament, problems remain with the meaning of the Old Testament prior to its being made part of a larger work that includes the New Testament.

Second, does the Contextual Approach help us deal with apparent factual errors in the Old Testament better than the Human Author Approach does? For example, that Adam lived to be 930 years old (Gen 5:5)? Or that fruit trees existed before the sun (Gen 1:11, 16)? The New Testament offers no reason to reject these claims (or to interpret them metaphorically), so the Contextual Approach seems to provide no help here.

Third, there is, I believe, a fundamental problem with the Contextual Approach insofar as it allows for metaphorical interpretations of passages meant literally by the original human author. Suppose a modern scholar, at the end of her career, republishes all her articles in a collection. She adds a preface indicating that she thinks some of her early works contain mistaken claims. Clearly, as we've already seen, this forces a new interpretation of those early works—they should, as part of the collection, not be understood as endorsing the mistaken claims. But suppose that, instead of admitting her mistakes, the scholar proposes that her early works should be given a metaphorical interpretation. I think we would rightly see this as an unjustifiable defensive move. Similarly, metaphorical interpretations of Old Testament passages which the original human authors meant literally seem to be unjustifiable. If this is correct, then wherever the Contextual Approach calls for a metaphorical reinterpretation of an Old Testament passage, it seems we must instead simply regard the passage as problematic. And a quick glance back at the list of problematic passages in the Old Testament (chapter five) indicates that, from this perspective, the Old Testament contains many apparent errors.

Fourth, does the Contextual Approach help us understand the problematic passages in the New Testament? We still have the apparent claim that the second coming of Christ will come shortly after the writing of Revelation and that a God of love will inflict eternal suffering on some people. Furthermore, does Jesus endorse the death penalty for cursing one's parents (Mark 7:9–10)? And what about passages that may seem to endorse slavery (Col 3:22) or assign women inferior roles (1 Tim 2:11–12)? Of course, the interpretation of these passages (or their status as problematic) may be debated, but the point here is simply that problem passages in the New Testament do not vanish simply by combining the Old and New Testaments into one book.

To sum up, unlike the Human Author Approach, the Contextual Approach does allow us to view many Old Testament passages as superseded by the New Testament. And it allows us to interpret problematic Old Testament passages figuratively. But it does not help with problematic New Testament passages. Also, the Old Testament apparently contained many problematic passages *before* being combined with the New Testament, so was it divinely inspired before being so combined? Finally, I have argued that the Contextual Approach is, in general, an unjustifiable approach to interpreting the Old Testament.

Let us turn now to some positive attempts to ground the claim that the Bible is divinely authorized (or that it is a divine revelation or a message from God).

12

W. J. Abraham's Approach

PHILOSOPHER WILLIAM J. ABRAHAM argues that God has given humans a capacity for recognizing revelation. He calls this capacity the *oculus contemplationis*—a contemplative or spiritually discerning "eye."[1] We may, upon viewing the starry sky at night, discern that a powerful intelligence created the universe. Or we may, through the deliverances of our conscience, discern that God is telling us what is right and wrong. Similarly, we may discern, by reading the Bible, that God speaks to us through it, revealing important truths.

Abraham is not saying that we obtain these truths first and foremost through reasoning or arguments.[2] Rather, spotting revelation is analogous to seeing something. For example, we see a person and know she's there; we don't argue for her existence—at least not typically. Similarly, with recognizing revelation: we spot it directly. That said, Abraham does admit that we need reasons or arguments to confirm what we learn through the *oculus*

---

1. Abraham, *Crossing the Threshold*, 66.
2. Abraham, *Crossing the Threshold*, 67.

contemplationis. Thus, in discussing a contemporary claim to divine revelation by a Mr. Hamza, Abraham says:

> To rest on his word alone is a very fragile foundation indeed. In challenging his claim [to possess a revelation], we are not pitting our finite minds against God; we are pitting our finite minds against Mr. Hamza's finite mind. To rely on his *oculus contemplationis* alone without additional support is to be at much the same level as resting on his word alone.[3]

So, Abraham is not claiming that the *oculus contemplationis* can adequately support a claim to revelation *all by itself*.

But one obvious difficulty here is that different people may "see" different revelations—or no revelation at all. Consider the diversity of religious beliefs among societies. For example, according to sociologist Rodney Stark, indigenous societies exhibit a wide variety of beliefs about God. Many such societies affirm the existence of a high god, a creator who presides over lesser gods and is concerned about human moral behavior (from 42 percent to 16 percent depending on the type of society, for example "nomadic" versus "slash and burn agriculture"). But many indigenous societies affirm the existence of a remote high god—a creator who is no longer concerned with his creation (from 22 percent to 27 percent of societies, depending on the type of society). Still others affirm no high god at all (from 36 percent to 57 percent of societies, depending on the type); these societies generally worship(ed) lesser gods of some sort.[4] So, it seems that if humans have an *oculus contemplationis*, the content of the revelation isn't very clear. Maybe the *oculus contemplationis* indicates only that there is some sort of reality beyond the range of sense experience.

And perhaps the *oculus contemplationis* can be blocked or interfered with in various ways. For example, perhaps the belief in a high god who cares about human moral behavior is burdensome. And perhaps polytheism is a less burdensome belief because the

---

3. Abraham, *Crossing the Threshold*, 150.
4. Stark, *Discovering God*, 59–61.

W. J. Abraham's Approach

gods of polytheism are less demanding.[5] Maybe so. Still, the *oculus contemplationis* doesn't seem to provide very clear and specific information, as compared with, say, vision. If the *oculus contemplationis* exists, it seems to lead (or allow) different groups to identify very different "revelations." And of course, many individuals would claim to discern no revelation whatsoever.

Notice that, as applied to sacred writings, Abraham's idea of an *oculus contemplationis* could apparently be used to claim that many books are divine revelations: the Qur'an, the Hindu scriptures, the Zoroastrian Avesta, the Book of Mormon, the Hebrew Bible, the New Testament, and so on. For each of these books, there is a group of people who see it as a revelation. Should we simply accept all of these books as divine revelations? Of course, they sometimes contradict each other, so we cannot consistently accept all that they tell us. But is there some way to discern when the *oculus contemplationis* is working well *in regard to a supposed written revelation* and when it isn't? By subjecting the various sacred writings to critical scrutiny? This might enable us to eliminate some candidate revelations. But it is far from clear that critical scrutiny would enable us to sort out veridical revelations in general from non-veridical pseudo-revelations (whether fraudulent or simply mistaken). Hard questions can be asked about the sacred writings of each of the major world religions. We apparently need some other way to confirm (or disconfirm) a revelation.

Imagine an animal whose light-sensitive faculty gives it only the ability to discern day from night. This animal's light-sensitive faculty does not reveal that trees exist. Or that tigers or tarantulas do. Is the *oculus contemplationis*, assuming it exists, rather like this light-sensitive faculty? If so, perhaps the *oculus contemplationis* tells us very little, just that there is some sort of reality behind or beyond the world we know through sense experience. As regards more specific claims, such as *the Bible reveals what God is like*, we would apparently need strong confirming arguments of some sort.

Then again, can we be sure the *oculus contemplationis* exists at all? No one doubts that many people have claimed to receive a

---

5. Stark, *Discovering God*, 96.

revelation. But this does not prove that there is a special human faculty for receiving revelations. In fact, many alleged revelations seem to be received through the conscience, through dreams, or through the senses (for example, seeing a miracle).

Consider an analogy. We often "sense" that a person we've just met is trustworthy (or, perhaps, untrustworthy). Does it follow that we have a special faculty for "sensing" trustworthiness, an *oculus-for-trustworthiness*? Or is it just that, because of our past experience, we can form such immediate impressions of others? Perhaps we pick up on some subtle visual or auditory clue that (based on past experience) signals something about the person's moral character. The point is that we should perhaps be wary of postulating a special faculty for each kind of impression (or intuitive judgement) we can form.

In any case, if we have an *oculus contemplationis*, it apparently does not provide us with very clear and specific information. And so, it seems we must rely *heavily* on whatever confirming arguments are available.

13

Reformed Epistemology

REFORMED EPISTEMOLOGY IS ROUGHLY the idea that human knowing is possible because God has given us cognitive faculties (such as vision, audition, and memory) that typically function well in the environment in which we've been placed. These faculties are designed to yield truth (for the most part) if used as God intended.[1]

The leading advocate of reformed epistemology is Alvin Plantinga. Here we are concerned with Plantinga's epistemology as it applies to beliefs about the Bible.

The fundamental idea in Plantinga's religious epistemology "is that God provides us human beings with faculties or belief-producing processes that yield . . . [central Christian] beliefs and are successfully aimed at the truth; when they work the way they were designed to in the sort of environment for which they were designed, the result is warranted belief. Indeed, if these beliefs are true and the degree of warrant sufficiently high, they constitute knowledge."[2]

---

1. Plantinga, *Warranted Christian Belief*, 156.
2. Plantinga, *Warranted Christian Belief*, 357.

Is the Bible the Word of God?

Warrant, for Plantinga, is that which, when added to true belief, makes it knowledge. To illustrate: I might believe that *Neptune is the eighth planet from the sun*, and my belief, though true, might be only a lucky guess and so not warranted. Or I might believe that Neptune is the eighth planet from the sun because I had a dream in which a talking frog said so, in which case my belief is not well grounded—not warranted. Finally, I might believe that Neptune is the eighth planet from the sun because I read this in a reputable textbook on astronomy, in which case my belief is warranted and counts as knowledge.

It is especially important to understand that warrant includes not only propositional evidence (arguments) but the grounding for properly basic beliefs such as *trees exist*, *I saw a deer yesterday*, and *1 + 1 = 2*. Properly basic beliefs do not need to be based on other beliefs in order to be warranted. It isn't always easy to specify the grounding for a properly basic belief, but here are some examples. My belief that *trees exist* is presumably somehow grounded in my sensory experience. My belief that *I saw a deer yesterday* is a memory belief. I don't have an argument for it, but when I consider this belief, it just seems to be true, and I have no reason to doubt it and no reason to think my memory isn't functioning properly. Presumably, that is all the grounding I need in regard to memory beliefs. In the case of *1 + 1 = 2*, the proposition just seems utterly obvious to me; I can't conceive any way it could be false; and that seems to be grounding enough.

From the standpoint of reformed epistemology, many religious beliefs are or can be properly basic. "Roughly speaking, he [the believer] reads or hears the central message of Scripture; [and] moved by the invitation or instigation of the Holy Spirit, he comes to believe."[3] In this way, specific beliefs such as *Jesus is Lord* become proper "starting points" for the believer. That is, they are *properly basic*: warranted without being based on arguments.

But, as Plantinga observes, "the traditional Christian also believes . . . that the Gospel of John and Paul's Epistle to the Romans and the book of Acts are divinely inspired and hence authoritative

---

3. Plantinga, *Warranted Christian Belief*, 375–76.

Reformed Epistemology

for Christian belief and practice. Indeed, he will believe this of the entire Bible."[4] And these beliefs also can be properly basic.

Some Christians may go through a process of reasoning about the Bible. For example, regarding the New Testament, some Christians might come to believe (1) "that the apostles were commissioned by God through Jesus Christ to be witnesses and deputies," (2) "that they produced a body of . . . teaching that incorporated what Jesus taught," (3) "that the New Testament books are all either apostolic writings or formulations of apostolic teaching composed by close associates of one or another apostle," (4) "that the process whereby these books found their way into a single canon is a matter of God's authorizing these books as constituting a single volume of divine discourse," and hence (5) "the New Testament is a single volume of divine discourse."[5] But according to Plantinga, premises (1) through (4) cannot be known through ordinary historical investigation.[6] Accordingly, if belief (5) is warranted for a person, it must be produced by the activity of the Holy Spirit. And in this way, the belief can be properly basic.

God has set things up so that humans are "wired" to believe what the Bible says *and* that it is the word of God. Why, then, don't all humans believe that the Bible is the word of God? The short answer is "sin and the effects of sin." But Plantinga puts the stress here not on sinful acts but on original sin, an orientation we are all born with. Our fallen nature, as humans, includes a tendency to resist the truth about God and God's will. We want to run our own lives rather than obey God. This orientation operates in subtle

---

4. Plantinga, *Warranted Christian Belief*, 376.
5. Plantinga, *Warranted Christian Belief*, 377-78.
6. Plantinga, *Warranted Christian Belief*, 378. Plantinga argues that even if the statements could each be shown to be probable, the conjunction of them would almost certainly have a low probability. To illustrate, consider a conjunction of four statements in which the conjuncts are independent (the probability of one does not affect the probability of another): A and B and C and D. And suppose each conjunct has a probability of ¾, or .75. The probability of the whole conjunction would be approximately .316, well below half. Thus, the negation of the conjunction would be more probable than the conjunction itself. (The math is a little more complicated if the conjuncts are not independent, but Plantinga argues the result would be similar.)

ways, even producing cultural factors that blind us to the truth about God, for example, alternate philosophies and tempting sinful lifestyles.

Now, it seems to me that Plantinga has shown how those who believe *the Bible is the word of God* might not only believe it but know it. This knowledge, however, depends on God's creative work. God must create humans with the right sort of cognitive faculties and place them in an environment for which those faculties are well suited. Has God done that? Christians may well believe he has, but is there any way to know it?

At this juncture, however, we need to keep an important epistemological point in mind. As Descartes noted long ago, all my sense experiences (visual, auditory, tactile, etc.) could conceivably be caused by a powerful evil demon out to dupe me and lead me into false beliefs. If an evil demon causes all my sense experiences, I might have many false beliefs. (For example, under such circumstances, even *trees exist* might well be a false belief.) Obviously, I cannot rule this demon possibility out by appealing to my sense experience. I can of course check some of my sense experiences by appealing to other sense experiences, as when I see a tree in front of me (a visual experience) and put out my hand to touch it (a tactile experience). But this procedure assumes that my tactile experience is veridical. At some point I must simply trust that my sense experiences are reliable (for the most part).

And, interestingly, there seems to be no way to test introspection at all. Suppose I feel a bit sad or anxious today. I take it for granted that I am a bit sad or anxious. There is no test to ensure that I'm correct as regards my inner states. Yet surely, I can know whether I'm sad or anxious on a given occasion.

It seems we must distinguish between knowing something and knowing that we know it. I know many things through my sense experiences. But if I'm asked to show that my sense experiences are generally reliable, I have no non-circular argument to provide. Any attempt to "prove" my sense experiences are reliable will involve an appeal to my sense experiences. So, if I want to avoid radical skepticism, I must assume that my sense experiences

Reformed Epistemology

are (for the most part) veridical. Similarly, through introspection I can know my inner states, even though I have no way to test introspection for accuracy.

So, could *the Bible is the word of God* be like *Trees exist* or *I feel sad*—something I believe because I'm "wired" to believe it in the right circumstances? Something properly basic for me—something I do not need to argue for? Yes, I think it *could* be like that. But there are questions to consider.

First, note that similar claims could be made for the Qur'an, the Zoroastrian Avesta, or the Hindu scriptures. Has Allah, or Ahura Mazda, or Vishnu "wired" people to believe that these books are divine revelations? It is hard to get beyond, "Well, that could be true." Should we believe that all these sacred books are divinely inspired or divinely authorized? Don't we need some evidence to sort these claims out? It seems to me that we do.

Second, the various sacred writings of the world religions contradict each other on certain matters. For example, the Qur'an tells us that Jesus did not die on the cross, contrary to what the gospels say: "And for their saying, 'We have killed the Messiah, Jesus, the son of Mary, the Messenger of God.' In fact, they did not kill him, nor did they crucify him, but it appeared to them as if they did" (Sura 4:157).[7] Is this disagreement about the death of Jesus a problem for the Qur'an or for the gospels? Or for both? The contradictory claims surely indicate that we cannot accept everything the Qur'an and the gospels tell us. But it seems that the Bible and the Qur'an are equally defensible as divinely inspired, from the standpoint of Reformed Epistemology.

Third, even properly basic beliefs can face *defeaters*, i.e., evidence that calls them into question. For example, suppose I'm driving down the road and see what I take to be an evergreen tree. I form the belief *I see an evergreen tree*. I don't argue for this belief; it's properly basic. But unknown to me, some kids are playing a

---

7. *Quran in English*, 42. See also the *Koran* (trans. Rodwell): "And for their saying, 'Verily we have slain the Messiah, Jesus the son of Mary, an Apostle of God.' Yet they slew him not, and they crucified him not, but they had only his likeness." *Koran*, 65.

Is the Bible the Word of God?

prank, and I find out later that the "tree" is not a tree at all but a papier mâché structure the kids have made. Once I'm informed of this, I cannot reasonably hang onto the belief that I saw an evergreen tree. And I should realize the belief is not warranted.

Are there defeaters for the belief that *the Bible is the word of God*? Here are some things to consider:

   a. A close reading of the Bible turns up many problem passages. I have provided a substantial list in chapters 5 and 6. Of special concern are those passages that depict God as doing or commanding or approving something that seems contrary to the claim that God is a God of love. Many people, upon reading those passages, find them quite troubling: "Would a God of love act in that way, or issue that sort of command?" For many people, these passages raise a question about the theological reliability of the Bible. Simply put, to many people, quite a few biblical passages do not seem like a message from a God of love.

   b. How plausible is it to suppose that people come equipped with a tendency, upon reading the Bible (or hearing it read), to believe it is the word of God? A series of questions need to be considered here:

      1. Roughly two-thirds of the world's population is non-Christian. Many of these non-Christians know something of the content of the Bible, yet they do not believe that it is the word of God. Why not? The reply will presumably be to remind us of the effects of sin, especially original sin, which can lead to the production of alternate philosophies and religions. Those in the grip of a philosophical or religious alternative to Christian faith are apt to resist (or suppress) the God-given tendency to believe the Bible is the word of God. But is this appeal to sinful human nature compelling? Is the production of alternate philosophies always a form of resistance to God? Don't honest thinkers simply tend to arrive at different conclusions when they try to understand the world and our place (as humans) in

it? *Also, might the adherents of other religions suggest that the shoe is on the other foot—that Christians are resisting the true message from God?*

2. From one point of view, the Bible is in effect a library of sixty-six books. And the books vary enormously in genre, style, and content. Even most believers will admit that parts of the Bible "leave them cold." They may read a number of biblical books with no tendency to form the belief that they're receiving a message from God—books such as 1 Chronicles, Song of Solomon, and Ecclesiastes. And in some other biblical books, readers may find that only a few passages seem to carry a message that is meaningful to them.

3. As is well known, many believers have never read much of the Bible and find it generally dull when they try to read it. So, is it really plausible to suppose that people in general are "wired" to believe the Bible is the word of God? *Even if the central message of the Bible is compelling to many, does that show that the entire Bible is the word of God?* Perhaps large parts of the Bible are not a message from God. And perhaps that's why so many people find much of the Bible dull and uninspiring.

Does reformed epistemology vindicate the belief that the Bible is the word of God? Certainly, God *might* have provided us with faculties that yield truth (for the most part) and which, when functioning properly, lead us to believe that the Bible is the word of God. That's a possibility. But, as far as I can see, reformed epistemology shows only that this is a possibility. And at the very least, we need to supplement this possibility with an explanation of why the numerous problem passages in the Bible do not defeat the belief that it is the word of God—especially those numerous problem passages that seem to many people to depict God as unloving or unjust.

14

Swinburne's Approach

RICHARD SWINBURNE ARGUES THAT there are four tests for revelation. First, the content must be appropriate. The "main point of a revelation is to tell us things for which we do not already have adequate evidence..."[1] God "is only going to intervene publicly in history to tell us things which are important for our deepest wellbeing and which we cannot find out with sufficient certainty for ourselves."[2] Second, a "purported revelation needs to be delivered in a way that God alone can deliver it."[3] This requires a miracle. For example, the resurrection of Jesus marks him off as an authentic messenger of God.

The "third test of a candidate revelation is whether the original revelation includes a revelation of how an interpreting church is to be constituted..."[4] Any revelation is subject to interpretation. So, "it must be part of a revelation that God will guide his church to

---

1. Swinburne, *Revelation*, 109.
2. Swinburne, *Revelation*, 109.
3. Swinburne, *Revelation*, 112.
4. Swinburne, *Revelation*, 122.

Swinburne's Approach

discover the correct interpretation of the prophet's teaching . . . ."[5] The "fourth and final test of a candidate revelation is whether the interpretations of it produced by the church provide the sort of teaching which God would have chosen to give to humans."[6]

Does the Bible pass the tests Swinburne proposes? And are Swinburne's proposed tests relevant and necessary?

The First Test. The Bible clearly purports to reveal important truths "which we cannot find out with sufficient certainty for ourselves." For example:

- The two greatest divine commandments are that we should (a) love God and (b) love our neighbor as ourselves (Mark 12:30–31; Deut 6:5; Lev 19:18).
- We should love (i.e., care about) even our enemies (Matt 5:44).
- We should forgive those who sin against us "seventy-seven" times (Matt 18:22).
- Jesus lived, died, and was resurrected to put us right with God (2 Cor 5:19).
- There will be a Day of Judgment (Matt 25:31–45).
- God offers us eternal life (Matt 25:46; John 3:16).

Thus, the Bible passes Swinburne's first proposed test.

The Second Test. Jesus' resurrection plausibly signals that he is an authentic messenger of God. But does it show that the Bible is a revelation from God (or divinely inspired, or authoritative)? Not directly. Jesus himself authored none of the biblical books (or any book at all).

But Jesus reportedly held the Hebrew Bible in high regard. For example, he reportedly said Scripture "cannot be set aside" (John 10:35 NIV) or "cannot be broken" (same verse, ESV). Also, "For truly I tell you, until heaven and earth pass away, not one letter, not one stroke of a letter, will pass from the law until all is

---

5. Swinburne, *Revelation*, 124.
6. Swinburne, *Revelation*, 125.

accomplished" (Matt 5:18 NRSV). So, Jesus apparently regarded the Hebrew Bible as, in some important sense, authoritative. But of course, he said nothing about the New Testament since it didn't exist during his life on earth.

Furthermore, how is the authority of the Old Testament to be understood, given the number of problematic passages, such as those listed in chapter five? The answer is by no means obvious. And a few New Testament passages seem to indicate that Jesus did not accept certain Old Testament teachings. Here are some examples:

a. The Old Testament distinguishes between clean and unclean foods and forbids eating unclean foods (Deut 14:1–21). But in the Gospel of Mark, we read, "[Jesus said] 'Don't you see that nothing that enters a man from the outside can make him unclean? For it doesn't go into his heart but into his stomach, and then out of his body.' (In saying this, Jesus *declared all foods 'clean'*)" (Mark 7:18–19 NIV, italics added).

b. In the Gospel of John, some Pharisees bring a woman caught in the act of adultery to Jesus (John 8:1–11).[7] The Pharisees point out that the Old Testament law requires that adulterers be put to death (Lev 20:10). How does Jesus respond? Famously, he says, "Let him who is without sin among you be the first to throw a stone at her" (John 8:7 ESV). And the accusers walk away. Now, if Jesus unreservedly endorsed the Old Testament law, why didn't he say something like "she deserves to die, but so does her partner. Where is he?" If the answer is that the Romans did not allow the Jews to practice capital punishment, then why didn't Jesus say something like this: "Of course she deserves to die. The law says so. But you know we can't stone her—the Romans won't let us. So, why bring her to

---

7. It is only fair to note that some of the best early manuscripts do not include this passage from the Gospel of John, e.g., Codex Sinaiticus and Codex Vaticanus (both dated 350 CE). But the passage is in Codex Bezae (dated c. 400 CE). Moreover, early church fathers such as Ambrose (c. 339–97), Jerome (c. 347–420), and Augustine (354–430) were familiar with the passage. See Wasserman, "Does the Woman Caught in Adultery Belong in the Bible?"

me?" Jesus' compassionate response to the woman in no way suggests that he thinks she deserves the death penalty; just the opposite: "[Jesus asks,] 'Has no one condemned you?' She said, 'No one, Lord.' And Jesus said, 'Neither do I condemn you; go . . . and sin no more'" (8:11 ESV).

c. In his Sermon on the Mount, Jesus says, "You have heard that it was said, 'An eye for an eye, and a tooth for a tooth.' But I say to you, Do not resist an evildoer. But if anyone strikes you on the right cheek, turn the other also" (Matt 5:38–39 NRSV). Is Jesus here calling into question Lev 24:19–20? "Anyone who maims another shall suffer the same injury in return: fracture for fracture, eye for eye, tooth for tooth; the injury inflicted is the one to be suffered" (NRSV). Since the Jesus of the gospels clearly in a sense resisted evil (e.g., condemning hypocrisy and destructive legalism, casting out demons, throwing the moneychangers out of the temple), he is apparently rejecting a certain common way of resisting evil, namely, the practice of returning evil for evil, of evening up the score, or paying wrongdoers back "in kind."[8]

So, Jesus' approval of the Old Testament does not appear to be a blanket approval. He sees the Old Testament as an authority but not as right on all counts. It is not to be read uncritically but with discernment.

Given that Jesus was resurrected and that he held the Old Testament in high regard, the Old Testament passes something close to Swinburne's second test. Jesus' authority is established by the miracle of his resurrection, and he approves of the Old Testament. Strictly speaking, this may not show that the Old Testament has been "delivered in a way that God alone can deliver it," but Christ's authority is established through something only God can do, namely, Christ's resurrection. And it is through Christ's authority that the authority of the Old Testament is confirmed—though (as we've just seen) Jesus apparently did not endorse *every*

---

8. I am indebted to Wolterstorff, *Justice in Love* (120–26) for my understanding of Matt 5:38–39.

Is the Bible the Word of God?

Old Testament teaching. Moreover, Jesus' endorsement of the Old Testament does not tell us how to interpret the numerous problematic passages within it.

Of course, the belief that Jesus was resurrected and that he endorsed the Old Testament depends on information found in the New Testament, especially in the gospels. So, from this perspective, the authority of the Old Testament presumes the general reliability (though not the infallibility) of the New Testament—or at least part of it. And we would need a separate justification for accepting the New Testament as divinely inspired or divinely authorized. (I'll return to this issue later on.)

The Third Test. Does the Bible meet Swinburne's third test? Does the Bible include a "revelation of how an interpreting church is to be constituted"? And does it reveal that "God will guide his church to discover the correct interpretation of" the Bible? Here again, an affirmative answer depends on the general ("for the most part") historical accuracy of the New Testament. The gospels indicate that Jesus spent a lot of time with twelve men to ensure that they understood his teaching. He promised them that "the Holy Spirit, whom the Father will send in my name, will teach you all things and will remind you of everything I have said to you" (John 14:26 NIV). He also instructed the apostles to "make disciples of all nations . . . teaching them to obey everything I have commanded you" (Matt 28:19-20 NIV). In addition, the New Testament (especially in the book of Acts and the Pauline epistles) gives us a picture of a community of believers forming around the teaching of Jesus, as interpreted by the apostles. Basically, then, the twelve apostles—guided by the Holy Spirit and teaching others, are the means of ensuring that the Old Testament is interpreted correctly and that as new writings become candidates for scriptural status (the gospels, Paul's epistles, etc.), they are vetted for reliability and interpreted correctly.

Do the New Testament books provide us with teaching that is true to the apostolic witness? Most likely, many churches regarded substantial parts of the New Testament (e.g., one or two gospels and most of Paul's epistles) as faithful to the apostolic witness by the end of the first century (or early in the second century), while there were still Christians who had themselves been taught by apostles and hence knew the apostolic witness firsthand. (I am speaking here of an informal acceptance, not of "official" acceptance in ecumenical councils. I have more to say about this later on.) This, I believe, provides some support for the claim that the New Testament books—at least the gospels and many of the epistles—provide teaching that is apostolic in content and spirit. Perhaps, then, the Bible passes Swinburne's third test.

The Fourth Test. Swinburne's "fourth and final test of a candidate revelation is whether the interpretations of it produced by the church provide the sort of teaching which God would have chosen to give to humans."[9] If we focus on the broad areas of agreement between Christians, as regards biblical teaching, Swinburne's fourth test seems to be met. Christians agree that God is almighty, just, and loving. They agree that God is the creator of "all that is, seen and unseen."[10] They agree that "God was reconciling the world to himself in Christ, not counting people's sins against them" (2 Cor 5:19 NIV). They agree that the two great divine commandments are "love God and love your neighbor as yourself" (Matt 22:36–40, paraphrase). They agree that Christ will one day judge "the living and the dead."[11] And so on.

But we must also consider the numerous problematic passages in the Bible and how they've been interpreted by the church(es). And here difficulties arise. For, as we've seen (chapters 5 and 6), many biblical passages seem to contain messages that a God of love would not choose to give to humans. These passages are understood in different ways within the community of believers, sometimes in disturbing ways that comport poorly with the claim that God is a God of love. Furthermore, in some cases, the Christian community *in general* has understood biblical teaching

---

9. Swinburne, *Revelation*, 125.

10. The wording here is taken from the Nicene Creed. Episcopal Church, *Book of Common Prayer*, 326.

11. Episcopal Church, *Book of Common Prayer*, 327.

to include claims that seem to run contrary to the law of love. Let me explain.

Nowadays Christians everywhere hold that the practice of slavery is wrong. But prior to the abolitionist movements in the 1800s, many Christians did not regard the practice as inherently wrong. And many Christians argued that the Bible permitted slavery, appealing to passages such as Eph 6:5, Col 3:22, and 1 Pet 2:18.

To this day, many Christian groups hold that women may not hold key leadership positions in the church, such as priest, pastor, and bishop. And these groups certainly claim that their view is supported by biblical teaching located in some of the New Testament epistles, for example, 1 Tim 2:11–14 and 1 Cor 14:34–35.

To this day, many Christian groups believe that God commanded the ancient Israelites to commit genocide—to slaughter the Canaanites—men, women, and children. And this belief is plainly based on an interpretation of certain Old Testament passages (e.g., Josh 10:40). Furthermore, the defense of this interpretation often involves the claim that almighty God can command anything he wishes, a claim which allows that, in principle, *any action whatsoever* could be morally required. And this defense carries with it the assumption that *God can act in very arbitrary ways—including ways that would not be loving—and still be worthy of worship.*

To this day, many Christian groups hold that God commanded the patriarch Abraham to sacrifice his son Isaac, based on their interpretation of Gen 22. Accordingly, Abraham was obligated to sacrifice his son. From this perspective, child sacrifice is not only permissible but a duty if God commands it. Of course, many Christians in these groups assume that God would not command child sacrifice today. But if God tested Abraham in this way, why not someone else? And if divinely commanded child-killing was a duty for Abraham, wouldn't it still be a duty today? In short, as many Christians interpret Scripture, they are led to allow that child sacrifice would be a duty under certain circumstances. Moreover, they are led to conclude that a God of love can command child sacrifice—after all, he once did so (they insist). But is this a

Swinburne's Approach

worthy conception of divine love? Or a conception in which divine "love" can be (and sometimes has been) highly manipulative? And a conception in which divine "love" can command cruel actions? (Surely, we would normally count killing one's son with a knife as a cruel act.) Accordingly, I suggest that the interpretive practices of many Christian groups implicitly undermine the claim that God is a God of love.

To this day, many Christians believe that during Old Testament times, the correct punishment for breaking the Sabbath, for adultery, for homosexual acts, for mediumship, and for striking or cursing one's parents was the death penalty. Such harsh punishment was morally right simply because God commanded it, and we know God commanded it because the Bible says so: Exod 21:15 and 31:14; Lev 20:9–10, 27, and 23:18. Once again, the interpretive practices of many Christian groups lead them to a conception of God that is unworthy. God's power trumps his love and justice, making the foundations of morality utterly relativistic.

Until fairly recently, most Christian groups have held very restrictive views regarding divorce, based on passages such as Luke 16:18 (NIV): "Anyone who divorces his wife and marries another woman commits adultery, and the man who marries a divorced woman commits adultery." While most people would agree that the breakup of a marriage is a moral tragedy, most would also agree that some marriages are on balance harmful (psychologically, spiritually, or even physically) for the husband, wife, or both. And yet Christian groups down through the ages have generally insisted that a husband and wife must stay together, with *very* few exceptions allowed. Beyond doubt, much human misery has resulted from the highly restrictive rules about divorce.

To this day, many (I think most) Christian groups hold that God will punish some people eternally in hell. Christians themselves often admit that it is hard to reconcile literally everlasting suffering with the thesis that God is loving and just. But their belief in eternal punishment is plainly based on their interpretation of certain New Testament passages, such as Matt 25:41–46 and Rev 14:9–11.

Is the Bible the Word of God?

Given the way Christian groups have interpreted problem passages, such as the ones listed here, it seems to me that *the community of Christian believers has often produced interpretations of the Bible that comport very poorly with the claim that God is a God of love.* Accordingly, I doubt that the Bible passes Swinburne's fourth test. It has too often been interpreted by Christian groups to mean something that implicitly undermines the claim that God is a God of love.

* * *

Now, let's take a step back and ask "are Swinburne's tests necessary and sufficient to establish that a revelation has occurred?"

Test #1. Regarding the first test, I think it would indeed be difficult to show that some proposition has been divinely revealed if it is something readily known through ordinary means, such as that the area of a rectangle is its length times its width or that the American Civil War began in 1861. A "prophet" who predicts that *the sun will rise tomorrow* will scarcely gain credibility when his prophecy is fulfilled!

Test #2. Must a revelation be "delivered in a way that God alone can deliver it"?[12] God might reveal his majesty through a person's experience of the starry night sky. God might reveal that a person's life has taken a bad turn through her conscience. It was revealed to Joseph in a dream that he should take his family to Egypt, though he had no miracle to establish that his dream provided a revelation. But to provide *publicly available evidence* that one has received a revelation, is a miracle needed?

We do see miracles used to authenticate a revelation in the Bible. Jesus' healings gave him credibility as a teacher of divine truth. Tongues of fire resting on the heads of Galileans who were preaching in languages they'd never learned gave the apostles credibility on the day of Pentecost. So, it seems that miracles *can* provide publicly available confirmation that a revelation has occurred.

---

12. Swinburne, *Revelation*, 112.

Swinburne's Approach

In the absence of a confirming miracle, the claim to revelation would apparently rest on the say-so of the claimant. And that is a very weak basis for belief. Some miraculous confirmation seems to be the only alternative. So, I think Swinburne is right about his second test. But it must be noted that people tend to be quite skeptical about accounts of miracles. So, confirmation by miracle requires very good evidence that a miracle has happened.

Test #3. Must an authentic revelation include content indicating "how an interpreting church is to be constituted"—a church that will arrive at correct interpretations?

All in all, I cannot see that a revealing God is required, as part of the revelation, to indicate how *a community that will provide correct interpretations of the revelation* is to be established. God might well leave interpretation—as he has left so much else—up to those who seek truth and goodness with intelligence, honesty, humility, and prayerful devotion. So, I doubt that Swinburne's third test is required of divine revelation.

One further thought is relevant here. Post-resurrection, Jesus might have written his own memoirs, and they might have included very clear and detailed accounts of his actions and his teachings. Or he might have worked with a biographer who could write a clear account of his acts and teachings (carefully edited and corrected by Jesus himself). Either memoirs or a biography could include Jesus' detailed views on problematic texts in the Old Testament. Works such as these might have been *far* less susceptible to misinterpretation than the Bible we have. And I think these possibilities are further reasons for doubting Swinburne's insistence that a revelation *must* include information about how an interpreting church is to be constituted. There are other ways of providing high degrees of clarity *if that were part of God's purpose.*

Test #4. Swinburne's fourth test involves evaluating whether the interpretations of the Bible "produced by the church provide the sort of teaching which God would have chosen to give to humans."[13] But since I don't think divine revelation must include a divinely appointed community of interpretation, I do not think

---

13. Swinburne, *Revelation*, 125.

there must necessarily be an evaluation of the interpretations of such a community to see if they exemplify "teaching which God would have chosen to give to humans."

To sum up, I find Swinburne's first test to be relevant and necessary in evaluating any purported divine revelation. A revelation must be of something we humans cannot discover by ordinary means. Swinburne's second test also seems relevant to me—and certainly helpful and even perhaps necessary. Without a miracle to confirm a revelation, we are forced to rely too strongly on someone's mere word. Finally, I do not think Swinburne's third and fourth tests are necessary. God isn't required to establish a community that will provide correct interpretations of a revelation. God might well leave (and, in my opinion, apparently has left) interpretation "up for grabs," with the hopeful result that intelligent and discerning interpretations will be widely accepted. Nor, in my view, does revelation require the existence of a community that has in fact consistently produced interpretations that comport well with the doctrine that God is a God of love. A community might well receive a revelation but fail to interpret it well. The Christian church has in fact—as I have argued—a very mixed record of interpreting the Bible.

The Bible certainly contains information that cannot be readily known through ordinary means. And Jesus' authority is confirmed by his miracles and especially by his resurrection from the dead—if the New Testament documents are to be believed. Jesus regards the Old Testament as in some sense authoritative. But he apparently doesn't accept all of it as true and he doesn't explain how we are to understand problematic passages. And so far, we do not have any support for the authority of the New Testament. How, then, can the authority of the entire Bible be defended (if at all)?

15

Prophecy and Biblical Authority

IN THIS CHAPTER I'M using the word "prophecy" to refer to *predictive* prophecy—prophecy that involves a prediction about the future. Of course, within the Bible, prophecy involves much more than prediction. The biblical prophets instruct people regarding the will of God, they urge people to obey God, they call attention to violations of God's law, and they call people to repentance.

If you search for "biblical prophecies" on the internet, you will find multiple websites claiming that fulfilled prophecies prove that the Bible is divinely inspired. Some sites say there are as many as two thousand fulfilled biblical prophecies! But if we take the trouble to look up the relevant biblical passages, many questions arise.

First, many of the prophecies are quite vague—the meaning is far from certain—so the claim that the prophecy was fulfilled by such-and-such an event is dubious at best. Second, in some cases the "prophecy" was apparently recorded *after* the event that allegedly fulfills it. In such cases, the evidential value of the "prophecy" is surely limited. Third, in some cases the alleged fulfillment is not plausibly anything the original human author (or his audience) would recognize as such. Fourth, in some cases, the prophecy is apparently false; it failed to come true. Fifth, not every book of the Bible contains predictive prophecy, for example, Ruth, Nehemiah, Esther, Job, Proverbs, Ecclesiastes, and Song of Solomon. Let me now expand on each of these points.

It has often been claimed that Gen 3:14–15 predicts that God will send a savior into the world. Here are the relevant verses:

> Genesis 3:14–15 (NRSV). "The Lord God said to the serpent, 'Because you have done this, cursed are you among all animals and among all wild creatures; upon your belly you shall go, and dust you shall eat all the days of your life. I will put enmity between you and the woman, and between your offspring and hers; he will strike your head, and you will strike his heel.'"

So, the offspring of the woman will strike the serpent's head, and the serpent will strike his heel. Is the meaning of this passage obvious? Couldn't the passage reasonably be interpreted as about the often-unfriendly relations between humans and snakes? To say the passage is *clearly* predicting that God will send a savior into the world seems to me quite a stretch.

It is often claimed that Deut 18:14–19 predicts the coming of the Messiah, an individual who will lead, save, and liberate the people. How clear is that?

> Deuteronomy 18:14–19 (NIV). "The nations you will dispossess listen to those who practice sorcery or divination. But as for you, the Lord your God has not permitted you to do so. The Lord your God will raise up for you a prophet like me [i.e., like Moses] from among your own brothers. You must listen to him. For this is what you asked of the Lord your God at Horeb on the day of the assembly when you said, 'Let us not hear the voice of the Lord our God nor see this great fire anymore, or we will die.' The Lord said to me: 'What they say is good. I will raise up for them a prophet like you from among their brothers; I will put my words in his mouth, and he will tell them everything I command him. If anyone does not

listen to my words that the prophet speaks in my name, I myself will call him to account.'"

These verses are meant to assure the Israelites that Moses is not the one and only prophet God will call. And the warning about sorcery and divination surely suggests that God will not leave the Israelites without prophets to guide them. But if the passage concerns only the Messiah, a single individual, then it concerns something that won't happen for over a millennium. (The exodus from Egypt is dated at 1446 BCE by some; others date it at 1225 BCE. Either way, there were over a thousand years between Moses and Jesus Christ the Messiah.) So, is the message of Deut 18 "don't worry, I'll send you a prophet like Moses 1000+ years from now. In the meantime, avoid sorcerers and mediums"? Spelled out thus, such a message surely provides little consolation for the Israelites of Moses's day.

In his magisterial work *The Promised Messiah*, James E. Smith observes that Old Testament scholars have "commonly stated that Moses is here [in Deut 18] predicting the rise of the prophetic institution which culminated in the Messiah. The term 'prophet' is here taken to be a collective noun embracing all the prophets from Moses to Christ."[1] And of course, God raised up many prophets in ancient Israel, including some of great spiritual power, such as Samuel, Elijah, and Elisha. It simply isn't clear that these verses in Deut 18 predict *the Messiah*—the unique future savior and liberator of the people.

Genesis 15 apparently gives a remarkably precise prediction:

> Genesis 15:13 (ESV). "Then the Lord said to Abram, 'Know for certain that your offspring will be sojourners in a land that is not theirs and will be servants there, and they will be afflicted for four hundred years.'"

---

1. Smith, *Promised Messiah*, 73. Smith himself takes exception to this common view, but if the passage is so clearly a prediction of a personal Messiah—a single individual, it seems odd that so many Bible scholars have failed to see this. Smith points out that Deut 34:10 says that no prophet "like Moses" has arisen, but he admits that "if these verses were written by Joshua as some think, then this assessment of the greatness of Moses was written before the rise of the great prophets of the monarchy period." Smith, *Promised Messiah*, 68.

Is the Bible the Word of God?

The Israelites were enslaved in Egypt for about 400 years (430 years, according to Exod 12:40-41). But when was Gen 15:13 written? We don't know for sure. But according to tradition, Moses is the author of the Pentateuch (the first five books of the Old Testament). Of course, Moses led the children of Israel out of slavery in Egypt. So, at least as far as we know, this verse was written *after* the period of slavery in Egypt, that is, after the event(s) that supposedly fulfilled the prophecy. (Here I am assuming that if Moses wrote Genesis, he wrote it after leading the Israelites out of Egypt—or at least that he could easily have edited or revised the manuscript after leading the Israelites out of Egypt, during the forty years in which the Israelites wandered in the wilderness). Thus, if we accept this as an example of fulfilled prophecy, we are demonstrating a very strong *prior commitment* to the trustworthiness of the Bible. The passage would hardly be accepted as an example of fulfilled prophecy by someone who lacked that prior commitment. To put the point bluntly, after an event is already known to have happened, anyone can make up a "prophecy" that supposedly predicted it would happen.

Now, let's consider some cases in which the alleged fulfillment is not something the original author (or his audience) would plausibly have had in mind. Consider this passage from the book of Psalms.

> Psalm 16:9-10 (NRSV). "Therefore my heart is glad and my soul rejoices; my body also rests secure. For you do not give me up to Sheol [the grave], or let your faithful one see the Pit."

In context, doesn't it seem that the psalmist is speaking about himself? ("You do not give me up to the grave.") He is expressing his trust that God is protecting him from an untimely death.

Psalm 16 is quoted in the New Testament as a messianic prophecy (Acts 2:25-27 and 13:35) which foretells the resurrection of Jesus Christ. But keep in mind two things. First, we are discussing prophecy as evidence for biblical authority. So, given the argumentative context, we cannot simply assume the authority of the New Testament. That would be begging the question.

Second, quotations from the New Testament do not necessarily tell us how Old Testament passages would have been interpreted by the original audience. And the psalmist is plausibly understood to be speaking about himself. Accordingly, I don't think we have a clear prediction of Jesus' resurrection in this psalm. In this connection, Old Testament scholar James E. Smith comments, "Only with the aid of the New Testament can the divine intention in many prophecies be ascertained."[2] But this underscores the fact that many Old Testament prophecies are unclear in their original context.

It has been claimed that Ps 41 predicts Judas's betrayal of Christ:

> Psalm 41:9 (NIV). "Even my close friend, whom I trusted, he who shared my bread, has lifted up his heel against me."

But once again, if we read the verse in context, the psalmist is apparently speaking about his own situation. In fact, on the face of it, he's not making a prediction at all but describing a past (or ongoing) event. Thus, Ps 41 does not provide a clear prediction of Judas's betrayal of Jesus.

It has been claimed that Ps 22 gives a detailed prediction of Christ's crucifixion. And of course, Christ quotes from this psalm in his agony on the cross: "My God, my God, why have you forsaken me?" (v. 1 ESV), but once again, the psalmist seems to be describing and lamenting his own plight. When he says "but I am a worm and not a man" (v. 6 ESV), it is natural to suppose that he is speaking about himself. Now, admittedly, to anyone who knows the details of Christ's crucifixion, the following verses are bound to strike a chord:

> Psalm 22:16-18 (ESV). "For dogs encompass me; a company of evildoers encircles me, they have pierced my hands and feet—I can count all my bones—they stare and gloat over me; they divide my garments among them, and for my clothing they cast lots."

2. Smith, *Promised Messiah*, 27.

Is the Bible the Word of God?

But still, in context, these verses seem to be describing mistreatment the psalmist himself received. After all, hands and feet can be wounded in many ways (including dog bites, spear thrusts, and knife stabs), not necessarily through crucifixion. And "evildoers" (criminals or enemies) have often stripped victims of their clothing. Furthermore, once again, the psalmist does not seem to be making a prediction; he's just describing something that happened to him. Finally, although parts of the psalm remind us of treatment Jesus received, other parts don't seem to reflect any events in his life—for example, "you have rescued me from the horns of the wild oxen!" (v. 21 ESV). So, do we have a clear prediction of Jesus' death in this psalm? It doesn't seem very clear to me.

In the Gospel of John (19:24) we read that, in dividing Jesus' clothing among themselves, the Roman soldiers fulfilled Ps 22. But again, bear in mind two points. First, in the argumentative context, we cannot simply assume the authority of the New Testament, for in doing so, we would be assuming the point to be proved. Second, it seems plain that the New Testament authors often operate with a rather loose notion of fulfillment: if an Old Testament passage calls to mind an event in Jesus' life, the Old Testament passage is said to be fulfilled—regardless of the natural interpretation of the passage *in its original context*. Obviously, a prophecy "fulfilled" in this sense has little or no evidential value.

Does the Bible contain any failed prophecies—predictions that did not come true? Apparently so. Consider these verses from the book of Jeremiah:

> Jeremiah 33:17–18 (NIV). "For this is what the LORD says: 'David will *never fail* to have a man to sit on the throne of the house of Israel, nor will the priests, who are Levites, ever fail to have a man to stand before me continually to offer burnt offerings, to burn grain offerings and to present sacrifices'" (italics added).

But the last Davidic king was Zedekiah, who was blinded and taken captive to Babylon in 586 BCE. (Jeremiah 52:11 says that Zedekiah was in prison till the day of his death.) And *even if* we count Jesus Christ as a Davidic king, there is a gap of about five hundred years between the end of Zedekiah's reign and the next Davidic king. That said, is it even plausible to suppose that Jeremiah had a *spiritual* enthronement in mind, as opposed to an earthly one? I don't think that's a natural interpretation of the prophecy.

Regarding Jer 33, Professor Smith asserts, "Jeremiah was not prophesying that the line of David would never be removed from the throne. That would contradict what he prophesied elsewhere concerning Jehoiachin: *Write this man childless, . . . for he shall not be successful in having one of his descendants sit on the throne of David or rule again over Judah* (22:30)."[3] But Smith's comment does not settle matters for two reasons. First, it presupposes that Jeremiah's prophecies are consistent. That makes sense if we grant that the Old Testament is infallible. But we can hardly assume the Old Testament is infallible when our question lies at a more fundamental level: "Why think the Bible is authoritative or divinely inspired?"

Second, Jeremiah uses the words "never fail." Never. But David did fail to have a man sit on the throne of Israel, for at least five hundred years. We aren't free to ignore the clear meaning of the words. As a comparison, imagine that Franklin D. Roosevelt, shortly before his death in 1945, had predicted that the Democrats will *never fail* to have a man in the White House. Would that prediction be true if the Democrats lost every presidential election for five hundred years and then began winning elections again? A "yes" answer is possible only if we empty the words "never fail" of their plain meaning.

Now, someone might claim that the prophecy in Jer 33 is *implicitly* conditional on the behavior of the kings (or the Israelites). But is that a natural interpretation? Notice that, if we do interpret the prophecy as conditional, its fulfillment is not remarkable at all: "There will always be a Davidic king—unless the kings or the people misbehave." After all, the Davidic kings and the Israelite people frequently misbehaved—egregiously! And so, assuming—for the sake of the argument—that the prophecy is conditional, it gives no assurance whatsoever that the line of Davidic kings would

---

3. Smith, *Promised Messiah*, 354.

never fail. But clearly, in context, the prophecy was meant to assure the people that the line of Davidic kings would not come to an end. *The prophecy surely wasn't meant to allow that, in all likelihood, the line of (earthly) Davidic kings will come to an end.*[4]

Let us now turn to some passages in the New Testament.

> Matthew 16:27–28 (NIV). "For the Son of Man is going to come in his Father's glory with his angels, and then he will reward each person according to what he has done. I tell you the truth, some who are standing here will not taste death before they see the Son of Man coming in his kingdom."

This passage seems to be about Christ's second coming and to predict that it will happen prior to the death of some of those to whom Christ was speaking. But the second coming didn't happen prior to the death of anyone in Christ's audience. Of course, one might produce some alternate interpretation of the passage, so that it is not really about Christ's second coming. But isn't the natural reading one in which the passage predicts the second coming? Many have thought so.

In a similar vein, consider these passages from the last book of the New Testament:

> Revelation 1:1, 4 (NIV). "The revelation from Jesus Christ, which God gave him to show his servants what must *soon* take place." And "blessed are those who . . . take to heart what is written in it, because *the time is near*" (italics added).

---

4. I don't deny that some prophecies are best interpreted as implicitly conditional. For example, Jonah proclaims, "Forty days more, and Nineveh shall be overthrown!" (Jonah 3:4 NRSV). But the Ninevites repent and so escape destruction. In the context of the story, Jonah's prophecy is a much-needed warning and hence best understood as implicitly conditional: "Nineveh will be overthrown unless the Ninevites repent." Within the story, the repentance of the Ninevites does not seem likely; it is unexpected, and Jonah is disappointed by it. He wanted the Ninevites to be punished. By contrast, given the history of Israel, misbehavior on the part of kings and their subjects is not unexpected but par for the course.

Prophecy and Biblical Authority

> Revelation 22:12 (NRSV). "See, I [the Lord Jesus] am coming soon; my reward is with me, to repay according to everyone's work."

> Revelation 22:20 (ESV). "He who testifies to these things says, 'Surely I am coming soon.' Amen. Come, Lord Jesus."

While "soon" is a vague word, is it plausible to think the human author of these passages had over two thousand years in mind? Would his earliest readers have understood him to mean that Jesus would return in, perhaps, a few millennia? Surely not. (The Greek words in the original are accurately translated with the English word "soon"—in a short time or without delay.) Accordingly, these passages apparently predict that Christ's second coming will occur shortly after the writing of the book of Revelation. And most scholars date the book around 95 CE. So, to all appearances, these passages are a failed prophecy.

Consider these passages from the gospels:

> John 14:13–14 (NIV). "And I will do whatever you ask in my name, so that the Son may bring glory to the Father. You may ask me for anything in my name, and I will do it."

> Mark 11:24 (ESV). "Therefore I tell you, whatever you ask in prayer, believe that you have received it, and it will be yours."

Are these predictions about prayer true? Even if we introduce qualifications (e.g., that we must not make selfish requests, such as the proverbial "dear God, please give me a bicycle"), how many Christians can *honestly* say that they've found these predictions to be true? How many Christians have prayed for the healing of a loved one, for protection from a natural disaster, or for the safety of travelers, only to find that what they asked for was not provided? These predictions about prayer just don't seem to be true.[5]

* * *

---

5. C. S. Lewis provides a thoughtful, clear, and honest discussion of these passages about prayer in "Petitionary Prayer."

Is the Bible the Word of God?

To this point, I've highlighted problems with the claim that *fulfilled prophecy establishes that the Bible is divinely inspired*. Many of the so-called fulfilled prophecies are simply too vague to count as such. And some "prophecies" were apparently written down *after* the alleged fulfilling event had already happened. Moreover, in many cases the alleged fulfillment is not plausibly anything the original human author (or his audience) would recognize as such. In addition, some biblical prophecies seem to be false; they are apparently failed prophecies. And if fulfilled prophecies are evidence of divine inspiration, failed prophecies would seem to count against it—*or at least they would qualify the sense in which the documents in question are divinely inspired*. And what about biblical books that contain no fulfilled prophecies, such as Nehemiah, Ruth, Esther, Job, Ecclesiastes, Song of Solomon, and Proverbs? The appeal to fulfilled prophecy leaves these books out. If they are authoritative or divinely inspired, there must be some other ground for thinking so.

Two additional points concern the logic of the appeal to prophecy. First, suppose a contemporary psychic were to make a few remarkable predictions that turned out to be true. Would this be good evidence that the psychic's pronouncements on moral, theological, and philosophical matters were, in general, divinely inspired or authoritative? I think the answer is plainly "no, it would not." The fulfilled predictions might lead us to have some respect for the psychic's teachings, but I think that few of us would assume those teachings were generally reliable, let alone infallible. The point of course is that there is a logical gap between making some true predictions and being a reliable source of truth in general.

Second, suppose an honest, competent, and careful journalist were to research a modern psychic's predictions, find that a few were true, and write an article reporting that the prophecies were fulfilled. Would this imply that the journalist's article was divinely inspired or authoritative regarding any theological or moral claims it contained? Surely, it would not. So, even if the New Testament accurately states that certain Old Testament prophecies were fulfilled, this does not logically imply that the New Testament documents are divinely inspired or authoritative regarding the theological and moral claims they contain.

All in all, the attempt to establish that the Bible is inspired by appeal to fulfilled prophecies seems to me well short of conclusive: (a) the argument *frequently* gets bogged down in matters of interpretation; (b) it overlooks some important cases of apparently failed prophecies in the Bible; (c) it ignores the fact that many biblical books contain no prophecy—and that others contain no *clearly stated* prophecies; (d) and perhaps most importantly, it misses the fundamental logic of the situation, namely, making some true predictions by no means guarantees that one's teachings are *in general* true or divinely inspired. Nor does accurately reporting on fulfilled prophecies guarantee that the report itself is inspired or divinely authorized.

16

Messianic Prophecy

Although I do not think that the appeal to prophecy by itself establishes the authority or inspiration of the Bible, I certainly do not deny that the Old Testament contains prophecies of a coming Messiah. And those prophecies could play a role in establishing that Jesus of Nazareth was the Messiah and hence a divinely authorized messenger. I now wish to provide a short summary of some of the clearer messianic prophecies. Let me emphasize that my purpose here is not to conduct a thorough exploration of messianic prophecies but simply to highlight some of the clearer ones.[1]

I begin my summary with this famous passage from Micah:

> Micah 5:2 (NIV). "But you, Bethlehem Ephrathah, though you are small among the clans of Judah, out of you will come for me one who will be ruler over Israel, whose origins are from of old, from ancient times."

This passage predicts the coming of a ruler of Israel. And the prediction is geographically specific: the ruler will be born in

---

1. For an exhaustive examination of messianic prophecies, see Smith, *Promised Messiah*.

Messianic Prophecy

Bethlehem Ephrathah. When King Herod asked for advice about where the Christ (Messiah) would be born (Matt 2:3), the Jewish scholars quoted Mic 5:2. Accordingly, "Without hesitation or debate the chief priests and teachers of the law pointed to Bethlehem as the birthplace for Messiah."[2] And of course, according to the Gospels of Matthew and Luke, Jesus was born in Bethlehem (Matt 2:1; Luke 2:4–18).

Next, consider this well-known passage from Zechariah:

> Zechariah 9:9 (NRSV). "Rejoice greatly, O daughter Zion! Shout aloud, O daughter Jerusalem! Lo, your king comes to you; triumphant and victorious is he, humble and riding on a donkey, on a colt, the foal of a donkey."

This passage occurs in a context in which the prophet seems to move quickly from prophecies about one place (or people) to another. Nevertheless, the passage certainly fits very nicely with the triumphal entry of Jesus into Jerusalem (Matt 21:1–11). Jesus rode a donkey on that occasion, indeed, a young donkey, a foal. The people cheered him on, many regarding him as the promised king (Messiah).

Notice, however, that both Mic 5:2 and Zech 9:9 (as well as many other passages, such as Jer 33:17–18) could naturally be understood as predicting the coming of an *earthly* king or ruler. So, is it surprising that the Jews of Jesus day expected an earthly Messiah? In this connection, J. E. Smith remarks, "The almost universal expectation was that the Messiah would be a temporal prince. Even the apostles were infected with materialistic notions of the kingdom until after Pentecost (Matt. 20:20–21; Luke 24:21; Acts 1:6)."[3] This highlights one way in which the messianic prophecies may be open to multiple interpretations.

Many consider the following passage among the most important Old Testament predictions concerning the Messiah:

---

2. Smith, *Promised Messiah*, 332.
3. Smith, *Promised Messiah*, 13.

> Isaiah 7:14 (NIV). "Therefore the Lord himself will give you a sign: The virgin will be with child and will give birth to a son, and will call him Immanuel [God-with-us]."

But at least two questions arise in regard to this prophecy. First, there is a debate about whether the Hebrew word translated "virgin" (viz., *'almah*) should instead be translated "young woman." Many English translations of the Bible opt for "young woman" in this verse.[4] Obviously, the difference in translation makes a difference. A virgin birth is a miracle, an ordinary birth is not. On this point, J. E. Smith states:

> Usage of the [Hebrew] word *'almah* prohibits thinking in terms of a married woman. If she is to be an unmarried woman, she would either be a virgin or an immoral woman. Since the birth of an illegitimate child . . . would not constitute then or now a very definite *sign*, one has to conclude that the *'almah* of Isaiah 7:14 is in fact a virgin.[5]

Here it should also be noted that the Septuagint translates *'almah* as *parthenos* (virgin). (The Septuagint is a Greek translation of the Hebrew Bible, believed to have been written by seventy-two Jewish scholars in the third century BCE.)

But a second question arises regarding Isa 7:14. Anyone who thinks this prediction is fulfilled by references to the virgin birth in the gospels (Matt 1:20; Luke 1:34–35) is plainly putting a very high degree of trust in the Gospels of Matthew and Luke. Just consider how you would respond to the report of a virgin birth alleged to have occurred in a nearby town last week. So, to show that Isa 7:14 is a fulfilled prophecy we would need *independent grounds* for thinking Matthew and Luke are *highly* reliable sources.

Multiple passages in Isaiah give glimpses of dramatic divine action yet to come, for example:

---

4. For example, "young woman" (instead of "virgin") appears in the following translations: the Revised Standard Version, New Revised Standard Version, New Life Version, New English Translation, Good News Translation, and the Common English Bible.

5. Smith, *Promised Messiah*, 252–53.

Messianic Prophecy

> Isaiah 29:18-19 (ESV). "In that day the deaf shall hear the words of a book, and out of their gloom and darkness the eyes of the blind shall see. The meek shall obtain fresh joy in the Lord, the poor among mankind shall exult in the Holy God of Israel."

> Isaiah 35:4, 5-6 (NIV). "Be strong, do not fear, your God will come . . ., he will come to save you. Then will the eyes of the blind be opened and the ears of the deaf unstopped. Then will the lame leap like deer, and the mute tongue shout for joy."

Jesus undoubtedly alludes to such passages in Isaiah when John the Baptist's disciples ask him if he is "the one to come" (the Messiah):

> Matthew 11:4-5 (NRSV). "Jesus answered them, 'Go and tell John what you hear and see: the blind receive their sight, the lame walk, the lepers are cleansed, the deaf hear, the dead are raised, and the poor have good news brought to them.'"

Thus, Jesus himself claims to be a living fulfillment of Isaiah's prophecies. And he claims that his ministry of healing indicates that he is the Messiah.

The following passages from Isa 53, regarding the so-called suffering servant, are among the most frequently quoted messianic prophecies.

> Isaiah 53:3-5 (ESV). "He was *despised and rejected* by men, a man of *sorrows* and acquainted with *grief*; . . . . Surely he has borne our griefs and carried our sorrows; yet we esteemed him stricken, smitten by God, and *afflicted*. But he was *pierced* for our transgressions; he was crushed for our iniquities; upon him was the chastisement that brought us peace, and with his wounds we are healed" (italics added).

Certainly, at the time of his trial and crucifixion, Jesus was despised and rejected by a great many people; consequently, he suffered greatly. According to the Gospel of John, he was scourged

Is the Bible the Word of God?

(19:1), and when crucified, he was pierced by nails (20:24–27), as well as by a spear that was thrust into his side (19:34).

The following verse from Isaiah provides more details about the suffering servant:

> Isaiah 53:7–9, 12 (ESV). "He was *oppressed*, and he was *afflicted*, yet he *opened not his mouth* ... By oppression and *judgment* he was taken away ... And they made his grave with the wicked and with a *rich man* in his death, although he had done *no violence*, and there was *no deceit* in his mouth." He "was *numbered with the transgressors*; yet he bore the sin of many, and makes intercession for the transgressors" (italics added).

Jesus was undeniably mistreated (oppressed and afflicted) by the Jewish and Roman authorities. And although Herod questioned Jesus "at some length, ... he [Jesus] made no answer" (Luke 23:9 ESV). Jesus' silence led Pilate to ask, "You will not speak to me? Do you not know that I have authority to release and authority to crucify you?" (John 19:10 ESV). Jesus was crucified along with two criminals ("numbered with the transgressors"). He was buried in the tomb of a rich man, Joseph of Arimathea. Jesus had harmed no one, and he had lied to no one ("there was no deceit in his mouth"). He prayed (made intercession for) those who tortured him: "Father, forgive them, for they know not what they do" (Luke 23:34 ESV). Thus, many events in the final days of Jesus' life fit very well with Isaiah's prophecy of the suffering servant.

Let's consider one additional, familiar messianic prophecy:

> Isaiah 9:2, 6–7 (NRSV). "The people who walked in darkness have seen a great light; those who lived in a land of deep darkness—on them light has shined. [. . . .] For a child has been born for us, a son given to us; *authority* rests upon his shoulders; and he is named *Wonderful Counselor, Mighty God, Everlasting Father, Prince of Peace.* His *authority shall grow continually,* and there shall be *endless peace* for the throne of David and his kingdom. He will establish and uphold it *with justice and with righteousness* from this time onward and *forevermore*" (italics added).

Messianic Prophecy

Here the prophet speaks of the birth of a most remarkable child. J. E. Smith explains:

> Isaiah speaks of the child's birth as though it had already occurred. The prophet, however, is certainly not referring to a past occurrence. No birth prior to Isaiah's time accomplished what is attributed to this birth. The interpreter is forced to the conclusion that the prophet is again employing *the prophetic perfect in which future events are so certain and so vivid to the mind of the seer that he can describe them as having already occurred* (italics added).[6]

The extraordinary child will—presumably as an adult—be an authority and his authority will expand continually. His reign will be one of endless peace. It will last "forevermore." This peaceful reign will be accomplished not by military might but by the moral virtues of justice and righteousness. The child will—again, presumably as an adult—be a wonderful, wise counselor. And more than that, he will be a divine being, "Mighty God."

The Christian church has certainly seen in this passage the description of no mere earthly ruler. What merely human, earthly ruler could ensure a peace that will last forever? What merely human, earthly ruler could secure endless peace by his moral virtue? And of course, no *merely* human, earthly ruler could also be divine.[7] The Mighty God is worthy of worship, and no mere human is worthy of worship.

Does Jesus of Nazareth, through his life and teachings, fulfill the messianic prophecies? This is of course a matter of debate between Christians and most Jews (namely, non-Messianic Jews). On the one hand, many messianic prophecies can be interpreted as involving earthly kingship, but on the other hand, as we have just seen, many of the prophecies do not seem to fit into that mold. Of course, Jesus himself reportedly said, "My kingdom is not of this

---

6. Smith, *Promised Messiah*, 264.

7. According to the Christian doctrine of the Incarnation, Jesus was both fully human and fully divine. For a discussion of theories of the incarnation, see Layman, *Philosophical Approaches*, 73–121.

world" (John 18:36 NIV). He saw his reign as spiritual and moral in nature.

Later I will argue that, from a Christian point of view, the authority of the Bible depends on the authority of Jesus Christ. If the events of Jesus' life match up well with Old Testament prophecies of the coming Messiah, would that be a line of support for his authority in spiritual and moral matters? I think it would be one line of support—but only one.

17

Curley's Reductio Revisited

PREVIOUSLY I SUGGESTED THAT any theologian or philosopher who wishes to claim that the Bible is the word of God must come to grips with Edwin Curley's reductio. It is now time for us to return to Curley's argument. Recall that it begins with these premises:

1. God is a supremely perfect being who possesses all perfections, including moral perfection.
2. The Bible is the inspired word of God.
3. In many places the Bible represents God as authorizing—that is, either commanding or giving permission for—conduct which is clearly morally wrong.[1]

Christian theologians in general accept premises 1 and 2. And since most people would agree that genocide is wrong, that child sacrifice is wrong, that it's wrong to give the death penalty to a son for cursing his parents, wrong to give the death penalty for adultery, wrong to give the death penalty to mediums, wrong to burn

---

1. Curley, "Reply to Van Inwagen," 85.

a prostitute to death (if her father is a priest), and so on, premise 3 is hard to deny.

But if premises 1 and 2 are true, it would seem to follow that:

> 4. The Bible does not seriously misrepresent God's moral nature by repeatedly portraying him as authorizing conduct he did not authorize.[2]

But don't statements 3 and 4 together imply:

> 5. God did repeatedly authorize conduct which was clearly morally wrong?[3]

And yet, premise 1 surely implies that:

> 6. God would never authorize conduct which is clearly morally wrong.[4]

Since statements 5 and 6 are logically inconsistent, we must give up at least one of premises 1, 2, and 3—or else we must reject one of the inferences made in arriving at statements 5 and 6.

In my view, the mistake in the reductio is the move from premises 1 and 2 to sub-conclusion 4: "The Bible does not seriously misrepresent God's moral nature by repeatedly portraying him as authorizing conduct he did not authorize." *The Bible—in many passages—does portray God as authorizing conduct he did not authorize.*

How can that be? How could writings that portray God as authorizing conduct he did not authorize be in some sense inspired by (or authorized by) God? How could such writings be God's word—a message from God?

First of all, why should God do anything through the agency of fallible and sinful humans? God can bring about effects through divine fiat and through created automatons. But God confers dignity on human beings by granting them important roles in bringing about his plans and purposes. So, why not simply create a

---

2. Curley, "Reply to Van Inwagen," 86.
3. Curley, "Reply to Van Inwagen," 86.
4. Curley, "Reply to Van Inwagen," 86.

flawless, inerrant book by fiat? For the same reason God leaves so many things up to imperfect human thinking, choice, and effort. God seeks to accomplish his ends largely through the free agency of fallible and sinful human creatures.

We can hardly expect a flawless, inerrant document if it is authored by fallible, sinful creatures who are deeply influenced by the morally imperfect culture they inhabit—a culture that may even be profoundly warped or barbaric from a moral point of view. God might well provide a human author with some insights and then let him develop his own work in his own way, be it history, epistle, prophecy, parable, law, poetry, or whatever. It would not be surprising if such a work contained profound truths but also errors and was therefore in need of being read with discernment and wisdom. *Such writings would be a word from God in the sense that a message God approves is available if the writings are read with appropriate discernment by the primary intended audience—the community of believers.*

One value of a fallible Bible is this: it tells us what people at various stages of moral development understood about God. It is important for us to understand that people inevitably view God through the lens of their own moral understanding. To the extent that the moral lens of a group of humans is malformed, cloudy, or otherwise defective, they are apt to get wrong ideas about what God is like and about what he requires and permits. That is part of our situation as human beings. We need to be aware of it.

Also, by including writings from cultures having deeply flawed moralities, the Bible vividly illustrates God's willingness to work with people in their present spiritual state, even if that state is morally barbaric. This divine generosity can come as spiritual comfort to those deeply aware of their own moral and spiritual poverty.

But doesn't this undermine the Bible as an independent guide to morality? Am I suggesting that we get to "pick and choose" the Bible passages we accept as true or authoritative?

Here we must remember that when we find certain Bible passages morally troubling, we do so because we are applying a moral

Is the Bible the Word of God?

standard that the church (the believing community) has arrived at, in large measure, by reflecting on the Bible as a whole. And, of course, the Bible contains many passages that people in general find morally insightful, compelling, and inspirational. To cite just a few examples:

- "Love your neighbor as yourself" is universally revered and plainly has implications for the whole of human life (Lev 19:18; Matt 19:19).

- A famous passage in the book of Micah provides a succinct and compelling summary of what a good God requires of human creatures: "And what does the LORD require of you? To act justly and to love mercy and to walk humbly with your God" (6:8 NIV).

- "As you wish that others would do to you, do so to them" (Luke 6:31 ESV). So many problems in the world would vanish if we all heeded this advice!

- In a world full of hatred and violence, Matt 5:9 gives a clarion call: "Blessed are the peacemakers, for they will be called children of God" (NRSV).

- Mark 7:21–23 (NRSV). "For it is from within, from the human heart, that evil intentions come: fornication, theft, murder, adultery, avarice, wickedness, deceit, licentiousness, envy, slander, pride, folly. All these evil things come from within, and they defile a person." The deep insight here is that a person's inner life determines her character. What we choose to dwell on habitually makes us the sort of persons we are.

- Galatians 5:22–23 tells us plainly the type of persons our Creator intends for us to be: ". . . the fruit of the Spirit is love, joy, peace, patience, kindness, generosity, faithfulness, gentleness, and self-control. There is no law against such things" (NRSV).

While passages such as these certainly do not give answers to all moral questions, they provide a moral vision that rules out many wrong paths that humans are prone to take. *Moreover, these insightful passages provide a moral vision that can guide us as we interpret the Bible as a whole.*

"Picking and choosing passages" fails to describe what's going on as discerning believers come to the Bible for moral guidance. It's more subtle than that. Here is an analogy. Sometimes when one is writing, one is unable to spell a word correctly. But if the correct spelling is provided, one can recognize it as correct. One isn't just arbitrarily selecting one possible spelling. One recognizes the correct spelling when one sees it—*even though one couldn't spell the word correctly on one's own.*

Another example. I may be unable to solve a story problem in a math book. But if someone helps me reason through the problem, I may be able to recognize the right answer. I can see the correct answer when it's provided, but I am unable to produce it on my own.

Yet another example. To complete a crossword puzzle, I just need one last word. But I'm stumped. Someone suggests a word and I immediately see that it works; it completes the puzzle.

A further point needs to be emphasized. When it comes to interpreting the Bible, we are not to operate simply as individuals—as "Lone Ranger" interpreters. The considered view of the larger Christian community must be taken into account. This serves as a corrective against idiosyncratic interpretations, of which, of course, there have been, and are, many.

An observation about the Old Testament is relevant here. I have listed many morally problematic passages in the Old Testament. But there is a feature of the Old Testament that makes it both inspiring and insightful from a moral point of view, namely, the numerous dramatic, morally insightful, edifying stories. And these stories are, for many people, more powerful as teaching tools than the relatively abstract content of the books of law (such as Leviticus and Deuteronomy) or even the epistles of the New Testament. Any Sunday school teacher will agree, I think, that it is far easier (and more fun!) to teach children the stories of the Old Testament than to teach lessons from the New Testament. Just to cite a few of the "greatest hits" from the Old Testament:

- The temptation of Adam and Eve. Something desirable (the forbidden fruit) may be a moral trap. And how readily we rationalize and fool ourselves (the serpent's role in the story). Moreover, bad things tend to result when we make wrong choices.

- Cain and Abel. We must be on guard against envy; it can easily lead to hatred, violence, and even murder.

- Noah and the Ark. Even if everybody else is behaving badly, one must do what is right.

- Jacob and Esau. How easily we can fall into unloving relationships, even with members of our family! But broken relationships can be healed through repentance and change of behavior.

- Joseph and his brothers. Even when bad things happen to us, we must stay faithful to God and to doing what's right. Also, God can work his good purposes even through the wrong actions of others. And ultimately, God rewards the faithful.

- The call of Moses. We are at times prone to belittle our talents and abilities, but God calls each of us to work for good, using the talents and abilities given us.

- Deborah the judge. God calls women as well as men to leadership roles. And sometimes we must take risks in service to God and the good.

- Samson the judge. A warning: great talent and promise can be lost through pride and through flirting with temptation.

- Ruth. Loyalty to friends and family is of great value.

- David and Goliath. Courage is a virtue; cowardice is a vice. Pride goes before a fall.

- Esther. Through the courage of one individual, a woman, a national disaster is averted.

- Jonah. When there is something God wants us to do, we may be tempted to try to avoid doing it. But trying to avoid it is not a good idea!

- Job. Life at times involves hardships and suffering, and it is tempting to blame God and to stop trusting him when hardships come. But we must trust God through good times and bad.

The point here is simply that, despite the numerous problematic passages in the Old Testament, it also contains valuable moral and spiritual teachings in the form of dramatic, edifying stories. These stories are among the most accessible and powerful teachings in the Bible. Arguably, the Old Testament stories reach children—and the child inside each of us—more effectively than the relatively abstract moralizing contained in other parts of the Bible.

To sum up, while the Bible contains many morally disturbing passages, if it is read with discernment by those who seek truth and goodness, it can provide a moral vision that is noble and inspirational—a vision that has in fact sustained faith communities over many centuries.

18

Summary of the Case for Biblical Authority

LET ME NOW BRIEFLY summarize my answer to the question: "Why think the Bible is a divinely authorized book? Why think the Bible is a message from God?"

My primary audience here is not atheists or agnostics but people who believe that there is an almighty God of love—and hence a God who might well choose to reveal certain important truths to human beings. The Bible obviously cannot be the word of God or a message from God if there is no God. And atheists and agnostics are apt to find much of the Bible literally incredible, given the Bible's frequent accounts of miracles and its claims regarding God's activity in creation and redemption.

We begin by reading the gospels, on the assumption not that they are divinely inspired but that they give a *generally* accurate account of what Jesus of Nazareth taught, what he did, and what he was like. This assumption of being accurate *for the most part* is one many of us make when we read ancient works of history that give the appearance of being an honest, reasonably careful attempt to provide a truthful account, for example, Thucydides's *The*

Summary of the Case for Biblical Authority

Peloponnesian War.[1] As New Testament scholar Craig Blomberg points out:

> Many readers assume that the Gospels narrate historical events simply because they read as if their authors are attempting to recount things that actually happened. The narratives are vivid but uncluttered, full of accidental details, ordinary people, and psychological realism, which set them apart from most ancient fiction and tendentious history."[2]

In short, the gospels purport to narrate actual historical events.

Many contemporary New Testament scholars, however, regard the gospels as highly inaccurate accounts, made up mostly of stories the church invented for its own purposes. This assessment rests on multiple factors, and while I cannot here explore them in detail, I want to characterize the four most important ones and suggest the direction a plausible response might take. I will focus on the Synoptic Gospels, Matthew, Mark, and Luke.[3]

First, there is skepticism about the accounts of miracles as incredible in a scientific age. But if one believes in an almighty God of love, this sort of skepticism is not well grounded. A God who created the entire universe can certainly perform miracles. And if a miracle serves God's purposes, he might well bring it about.

Second, there is the hermeneutic of suspicion. As New Testament scholar N. T. Wright comments:

> The guild of New Testament studies has become so used to operating with a hermeneutic of suspicion that we find ourselves trapped in our own subtleties. If two ancient writers agree about something, that proves one got it from the other. If they seem to disagree, that proves that

---

1. Thucydides was probably born around 460 BCE and fought as a general in one phase of the Peloponnesian War, the great war between Athens and Sparta (431–34 BCE).

2. Blomberg, *Reliability of the Gospels*, 196.

3. The Gospel of John raises special questions because it is very different from Matthew, Mark, and Luke. Nevertheless, Craig Blomberg provides a plausible defense of the historical reliability of John. See Blomberg, *Reliability of the Gospels*, 196–240.

Is the Bible the Word of God?

one or both are wrong. If they say an event fulfilled biblical prophecy, they made it up to look like that. If an event or saying fits a writer's theological scheme, that writer invented it.[4]

The fundamental problem with the hermeneutic of suspicion is that it is contrary to sound historical method. We must begin by giving the author the benefit of the doubt. In other words, we need solid evidence to reject what an author is claiming, rather than demanding proof that the author is correct. *And mere suspicion is not evidence.*

Consider an analogy I've used previously. Descartes pointed out that a powerful demon could conceivably cause all my sense experiences. I can't disprove this possibility by appealing to my sense experiences; they are all in question on Descartes's hypothesis. Rather, I must begin by trusting my sense experiences and doubt them only when there are specific reasons to do so. For example, a pencil looks bent when placed in a glass of water, but it feels straight. In this case, my tactile experience gives me good reason to doubt my visual experience.

If we demand proof that an author is providing accurate historical information, we are apt to wind up as "history skeptics" because often, no such proof is available. (The so-called "proof" would usually be the claims of another author writing in the same period. While it is of course helpful to have confirmation from multiple authors, as regards ancient authors, it is often nonexistent.) As in the case of our sense experience, we must begin by giving the benefit of the doubt. We should reject what the author says only when we have specific, solid grounds for doing so.

Third, it is claimed that the gospels often contradict each other; hence, they contain many false claims and are unreliable as history. It is impossible to explore this issue in detail here, but let me illustrate why I think this objection is overdrawn:

- In many cases the chronologies of the gospels differ. For example, Mark has Jesus recruit Peter, James, and John

4. Wright, "Knowing Jesus," 18.

very early in his account (1:16–20), while Luke places this recruiting event later on (5:1–11). But while modern readers tend to expect strict chronology in historical writings, ancient authors felt free to arrange their histories topically. And Luke may have placed the call of Peter, James, and John later to avoid an impression Mark may give, namely, that "the disciples' decision to join Jesus was more spontaneous and unmotivated than it actually was."[5]

- Mark and Luke seem to forbid divorce and remarriage for any reason (Mark 10:11–12; Luke 16:18), while Matthew allows an exception in the case of adultery (Matt 19:9). But it's quite possible that Mark and Luke are just not bothering to mention an exception that their audiences would have taken for granted.[6] Pithy sayings often allow for unstated exceptions.

- The genealogies of Jesus in Matthew (1:2–17) and Luke (3:23–36) differ significantly. But it may well be that Matthew is giving Joseph's ancestry while Luke is giving Mary's.[7]

- In some cases, one gospel mentions two characters in an episode while another gospel mentions only one character. Thus, Mark mentions only one Gadarene demoniac (5:1–20), while Matthew mentions two (8:28–34). But in such cases, it might be that one of the characters was dominant in the episode, and so the other character is "easily ignored in narratives that regularly omitted non-essential details."[8] (Here it might be useful to think of a time when you were called on to give a short version of an adventure or major decision in your life. You likely left some things out but still managed to capture the most important parts of the account.)

- Now, there do seem to be some clear contradictions between the gospel accounts. For example, the gospels tell us that two criminals were crucified alongside Jesus, one on his right,

---

5. Blomberg, *Reliability of the Gospels*, 169.
6. Blomberg, *Reliability of the Gospels*, 173.
7. Blomberg, *Reliability of the Gospels*, 193.
8. Blomberg, *Reliability of the Gospels*, 194.

the other on his left. But Mark says, "Those who were crucified with him also reviled him" (15:32 NRSV), while Luke indicates that only one of the criminals "railed at him"—the other criminal was repentant (23:39–43). Luke may have had a source (oral or written) that Mark lacked. In any case, this sort of difference is obviously minor and hardly suggests that either Mark or Luke fail to provide an account that is *generally* accurate. Moreover, such relatively minor discrepancies provide evidence that the gospel writers did not collude to harmonize their accounts.

To sum up, many of the so-called contradictions among the gospels probably do not indicate any significant disagreement. Furthermore, even if there is occasional disagreement among the gospel authors, while this would indicate some error, it would not show that the gospels fail to provide generally accurate accounts of Jesus' life and teachings.[9]

Fourth, some authors have suggested that the New Testament we have is greatly altered from the original manuscripts, because of multiple copying errors.[10] But, as F. F. Bruce observes, the "evidence for our New Testament writings is ever so much greater than the evidence for many writings of classical authors, *the authenticity of which no one dreams of questioning*" (italics added).[11] Consider the following examples:[12]

- Thucydides, *The Peloponnesian War*, was written roughly 400 years BCE. The earliest available manuscript is dated around 900 CE.

---

9. Holden and Geisler, *Handbook of Archaeology and the Bible* (143–58), provide a detailed discussion of alleged contradictions among the gospels. In my view, these authors succeed in showing that most of these allegations fall apart under scrutiny.

10. For example, Ehrman, *Misquoting Jesus*.

11. Bruce, *New Testament Documents*, 15.

12. Bruce, *New Testament Documents*, 16. The same dates are given by Holden and Geisler, *Handbook of Archaeology and the Bible*, 129, except in the case of Tacitus's *Annals*. These authors date the earliest manuscript of the *Annals* at 1100 CE.

Summary of the Case for Biblical Authority

- Caesar's *Gallic War* was written between 58 and 50 BCE. The oldest available manuscript is dated about 900 years later.
- Tacitus, *The Annals of Imperial Rome*, was written between 105 and 120 CE. The earliest manuscript of *The Annals* is dated around 900 CE.

Classical scholars do not, in general, doubt that we have fairly accurate copies of these works. Compare a small sample of the textual attestation for the New Testament.[13] (Keep in mind that the New Testament documents were written sometime between 50 and 100 CE.)

- Codex Vaticanus and Codex Sinaiticus are dated around 350 CE. (A codex is in the form of a book rather than a scroll.) These two codices are generally considered the best manuscripts available.
- The Chester Beatty Papyri I, which contains large portions of all four gospels and Acts, is dated sometime between 200 and 300 CE.

In short, the textual attestation for the New Testament is far superior to that of many classical works. Simply put, if we reasonably believe we know what Thucydides, Caesar, and Tacitus said, we can reasonably believe we know what the New Testament authors said.

Very well. I've now sketched my reasons for assuming the gospels are *for the most part* historically reliable. (I am certainly not claiming that they are entirely without error.) So, I shall now proceed on the assumption that the gospels are, generally speaking, reliable.

The Jesus of the gospels is an insightful teacher who claims to be speaking for God. His central moral teaching is "love God and love your neighbor as yourself." Through his thought-provoking

---

13. Bruce, *New Testament Documents*, 16–17. See also Holden and Geisler, *Handbook of Archaeology and the Bible*, 119, 121. Small fragments of the New Testament, such as the John Rylands fragment, are dated as early as 117–38 CE, according to Holden and Geisler.

parables, such as the prodigal son and the good Samaritan, he emphasizes both God's love and the kind of love (or caring) we should have for others. Jesus embodies holy love in his own character. He works miracles of healing and other miracles, such as feeding the five thousand. He comes into conflict with the religious authorities over matters such as healing on the Sabbath and driving the moneychangers out of the temple. He claims to be the promised Messiah. He is crucified, apparently for alleged blasphemy. He dies but does not stay dead. He is resurrected and appears to his disciples on multiple occasions.

Based on the account in the gospels, we may reasonably judge Jesus to be an authentic messenger of God. Accordingly, we take his teaching to be authoritative. And in his teaching, he frequently appeals to passages from the Old Testament. He plainly treats the Old Testament books as in some sense authoritative:

- Matthew 5:17 (NIV). "Do not think that I have come to abolish the Law or the Prophets; I have not come to abolish them but to fulfill them."

- Matthew 4:4 (NRSV). "But he [Jesus] answered, 'It is written, *One does not live by bread alone, but by every word that comes from the mouth of God.*'" (Jesus is here quoting Deut 8:3).

- Luke 10:25–28 (NRSV). "Just then a lawyer stood up to test Jesus. 'Teacher,' he said, 'what must I do to inherit eternal life?' He [Jesus] said to him, 'What is written in the law? What do you read there?' He [the lawyer] answered, 'You shall love the Lord your God with all your heart, and with all your soul, and with all your strength, and with all your mind; and your neighbor as yourself.' And he [Jesus] said to him, 'You have given the right answer; do this, and you will live.'"

- Matthew 22:29 (NIV). "Jesus replied, 'You are in error because you do not know the Scriptures or the power of God.'"

- John 10:35 (NRSV). "[Jesus answered, . . .] the scripture cannot be annulled."

Summary of the Case for Biblical Authority

As New Testament scholar F. F. Bruce comments, "When we think of Jesus and his Palestinian apostles . . . we may be confident that they agreed with contemporary leaders in Israel about the contents of the canon."[14] And the church, the community of Jesus' disciples, follows Jesus in regarding the Old Testament as authoritative. This does not imply that the Old Testament is without error. First, as previously noted, Jesus himself apparently took exception to certain Old Testament teachings. For example, he declared all foods clean (Mark 7:19), contrary to Old Testament law (Deut 14:1–21). And in the famous incident with the woman caught in adultery (John 8:1–11), his responses strongly suggest that he does not endorse the death penalty for adultery. Furthermore, in Matt 5:38–39, Jesus apparently rejects the lex talionis (the "eye for an eye" principle). Thus, Jesus read the Old Testament critically, and so should we.

In this connection, it is important to bear in mind that, as humans, we are used to regarding sources as authoritative but fallible. Most of what we know is learned through fallible authorities such as encyclopedias, textbooks, maps, journalists, medical doctors, and so on.

Second, Christians are to read the Old Testament in the light of the New Testament. In the character and teaching of Jesus, we learn what God is like and how God wants us to live. Thus, we may rightly question any Old Testament teaching that comports poorly with what we learn from Jesus. And "what we learn from Jesus" includes all the books of the New Testament, if (a) they accurately reflect apostolic teaching and (b) the apostles were faithful in conveying what they learned from Jesus.

---

14. Bruce, *Canon of Scripture*, 41. The Hebrew Bible is organized a bit differently than the Christian Old Testament. There are three main divisions in the Hebrew Bible. (1) Torah (law): Genesis, Exodus, Leviticus, Numbers, and Deuteronomy. (2) The Prophets, subdivided into the former prophets (Joshua, Judges, Samuel, and Kings) and the latter prophets (Isaiah, Jeremiah, Ezekiel, and the twelve so-called minor prophets). (3) The Writings. First come Psalms, Proverbs, and Job; then Song of Songs, Ruth, Lamentations, Ecclesiastes, Esther; and finally, Daniel, Ezra-Nehemiah, and Chronicles. See Bruce, *Canon of Scripture*, 29.

Is the Bible the Word of God?

Jesus selected twelve men, whom we call apostles, and spent about three years teaching and training them. Thus, as the early church came into being and grew in numbers, the apostles were the best available sources regarding the life and teaching of Jesus.

The book of Acts provides important information regarding the activity of the apostles after Jesus' death. On the day of Pentecost, fifty days after the Passover (the time of Jesus' death), the apostles preached the gospel in a variety of languages to people in Jerusalem (Acts 2:1-15). About three thousand people were baptized that day (Acts 2:41). Acts also tells us that the apostles:

- Worked "many wonders and signs" (Acts 2:43 NRSV).

- Were arrested by the authorities (Acts 5:18) but were released after being beaten (5:40).

- Led the church to appoint seven men to distribute food to needy members, so that they—the twelve apostles—could devote themselves to "preaching the word of God" (Acts 6:1-6 ESV).

- Were present as crucial decisions were made concerning preaching the gospel to gentiles (Acts 11:1; 15:6).

The book of Acts focuses mostly on the work of Peter and Paul, but the apostle John appears by name (Acts 3:3-11; 4:13-22; 8:14), and we are told that James—the brother of John and also an apostle—was martyred (Acts 12:2). Although Acts focuses on Peter and Paul, it does tell us (as indicated above) that the twelve apostles were active in spreading the gospel and in nurturing the community of believers in its infancy.

By instructing the apostles with care over several years, Jesus in effect transferred his authority to them. So, if we accept that Jesus was a divinely authorized teacher and messenger, that divine authorization transfers to his apostles. And the church selected the books of the New Testament on the grounds that they reflect the teaching of the apostles. As biblical scholar F. F. Bruce puts it:

> One thing must be emphatically stated. The New Testament books did not become authoritative for the Church

Summary of the Case for Biblical Authority

> because they were formally included in a canonical list; on the contrary, the Church included them in her canon because she already regarded them as divinely inspired, recognising their *innate worth and general apostolic authority*, direct or indirect (italics added).[15]

After all, the members of the early church did not want to follow a fictitious character; they sought to follow Jesus of Nazareth. And the apostles were the recognized authorities regarding Jesus—what he did, what he taught, and what he was like as a person.

So, if we trust the New Testament as authoritative, it is because the church, early on, accepted most of the New Testament books as true to apostolic teaching. New Testament scholar Bruce Metzger stresses the church's early acceptance of most of the books of the New Testament:

> During the course of the second century most churches came to possess and acknowledge a canon which included the present four Gospels, the Acts, thirteen letters of Paul, I Peter, and I John. Seven books still lacked general recognition; Hebrews, James, II Peter, II and III John, Jude, and Revelation.[16]

And there is little doubt that many of the New Testament writings circulated among the churches within years of their authorship. This means that many of these documents were circulating among the churches while the apostles and/or those who had been taught directly by the apostles were still alive. For example, Paul's first letter to the Thessalonians was likely written in 51 CE, only about twenty years after Jesus was crucified. Paul's letter to the Romans was probably written in 57 CE. The dates scholars assign to the Synoptic Gospels—Matthew, Mark, and Luke—vary widely but generally lie between 50 CE and 90 CE.

Here's an illustration to make these ideas more concrete. An apostle who was, say, thirty, at the time of Jesus' crucifixion (about

---

15. Bruce, "Canon of the New Testament," 9–10. A writing would have "indirect" apostolic authority if it accurately reflects apostolic teaching but is not written by an apostle, e.g., the Gospel of Mark or Gospel of Luke.

16. Metzger, "Formation of the New Testament Canon," 11.

Is the Bible the Word of God?

30 CE), would be seventy years old in 70 CE. Thus, many people who were taught directly by an apostle would presumably still be alive by the end of the century. For example, suppose Julia (a hypothetical first-century convert to Christianity) was born in 40 CE and taught by an apostle when she was twenty years old and he was sixty. Julia herself would of course be sixty at the end of the century. Christians such as Julia would be in a good position to assess whether a document was faithful to apostolic teaching.

Regarding the early circulation of New Testament writings, it is interesting to note a passage in the second epistle of Peter:

> Second Peter 3:15–16 (NIV). "Bear in mind that our Lord's patience means salvation, just as our dear brother Paul also wrote you with the wisdom that God gave him. He writes the same way in all his letters, speaking in them of these matters. His letters contain some things that are hard to understand, which ignorant and unstable people distort, *as they do the other Scriptures*, to their own destruction" (italics added).

The date of authorship of 2 Peter is disputed. If the apostle Peter wrote the letter, it would be dated in the 60s CE (since Peter is thought to have been martyred during Nero's reign). Many scholars suggest a later date, such as 80–90 CE, in which case the letter is pseudepigraphal. *But the crucial thing to note is this: the author regards Paul's epistles as Scripture and he assumes his audience is aware of Paul's epistles.*[17]

To be clear, the claim is not that the New Testament books were written by the twelve apostles. Some of the books may have been by apostles, for example, the Gospel of Matthew and the Gospel of John. But some were not written by apostles, such as the Gospel of Luke and the Gospel of Mark. The claim is rather that the gospels and the Pauline Epistles are true to apostolic teaching.[18]

---

17. For the date of authorship of 2 Peter, see Green, *Second Epistle General of Peter*, 13–48. Green shows, I think, that the earlier date of authorship (in the sixties) is defensible, though not certain.

18. Paul is an apostle but not one of the original twelve apostles. The book of Acts makes clear, however, that Paul's teaching had the approval of the

Summary of the Case for Biblical Authority

Keep in mind that the apostles were active as teachers in the early church, and so many of the earliest Christians knew of apostolic teaching firsthand, could pass it along to others, and could detect clear departures from it.

The authority of the New Testament rests on the discernment of the early church. If we trust the New Testament as a reliable account of apostolic teaching, we do so because the early church regarded it as such. Our faith is in part faith in the early church.

Christians believe that the Holy Spirit guided the early church as it selected those documents that best reflected apostolic teaching. But of course, the work of the Spirit is not open to empirical observation. We can say, however, that the New Testament books have served to inspire, instruct, edify, and strengthen communities of faith from the earliest Christian times to the present.

Let me add two points of clarification. First, it took many years for the church to settle on a formal decision about the full list of books in the New Testament. (There are twenty-seven books in the New Testament altogether.) The official decision by church councils came late in the 300s. But most of the twenty-seven books had long since been informally accepted as authoritative by most of the churches. Second, while the argument I've summarized here for the authority of the New Testament is, in my view, the best one available, it does not support the claim that the New Testament is an infallible authority. And obviously, this makes a big difference when it comes to interpreting the New Testament.

My argument has three key premises. First, Jesus was a prophet, a divinely approved authority. This we can accept if we accept the gospels as generally accurate accounts of his actions, his teaching, his death, and his resurrection. Second, the apostles provided generally accurate accounts of Jesus' actions, teaching, death, and resurrection. Of course, we have no way to compare the apostles' account with any independent account of what Jesus said and did. But my claim is that it is reasonable to assume that the apostles provide us with a generally accurate account of Jesus because (a) we can reasonably believe that Jesus devoted himself

---

twelve apostles (Acts 9:27–30; 11:19–30; 13:1–3).

to teaching and training the apostles and (b) we can reasonably believe that they remained devoted to him because of their role in starting and nurturing the church (the community of believers in Jesus). Third, we can reasonably believe that the church adopted the books of the New Testament *because the church judged that the books were faithful to apostolic teaching* (as well as edifying). Thus, the authority of Jesus is transferred to the New Testament books by way of the apostles and the discernment of the church.

One point needs to be emphasized. Christians are not in the position of simply accepting one man's claim to be a prophet or messenger of God. According to the gospel writers, Jesus' teaching, actions, and miracles were witnessed by many others, especially by the twelve apostles. If the gospels are generally accurate accounts, they provide substantial evidence for the belief that Jesus was an authentic messenger of God.

In what sense is the Bible the word of God or a message from God? Many have assumed that the human authors of the Bible were guided in a direct way by the Holy Spirit. While God may indeed at times have directly guided the Bible authors, I find it plausible to suppose that, for the most part, the books of the Bible are examples of appropriated or deputized writing. Through the church God has selected the books but has allowed the human authors to speak for him. Given the fallibility of the human authors, however, it is vital to keep in mind that the biblical writings must be read with discernment. Only what is consistent with God's love and justice can rightly be understood to be a message from God. *We should read the Bible seeking not simply what the human authors said or meant but seeking to discern the message a God of holy love communicates through them.*

Now, however, we must consider objections to the claim that the Bible is a message from God or that it is a divinely authorized source of truths regarding God and how God wants us to live.

19

Problematic Divine Commands

THE PROBLEM PASSAGES IN *the Bible do not involve trivial matters. For example, a God who commands genocide, child sacrifice, and the death penalty for cursing one's parents seems, to many people, unjust and unloving. Thus, the Bible is readily understood to be giving a false impression of God if God is indeed loving and just.*

It is true that parts of the Bible describe God as commanding actions that are plausibly (plainly?) inconsistent with love and justice. Here, I can only repeat a point made previously. If God chooses to reveal truths through human authors, the result is apt to be a mix of insights and errors. Authors writing under the influence of a morally barbaric culture are very likely to think God sometimes approves of actions that are unjust and/or unloving.

Experience indicates that it is tempting for human beings to believe that God is on their side in time of war and that it is also tempting to believe that mass slaughter is the best approach in warfare. For example, less than two hundred years ago, relatively few white Americans apparently had any qualms about slaughtering entire tribes of native Americans. And during WWII, America

Is the Bible the Word of God?

firebombed sixty-seven Japanese cities, killing tens of thousands of Japanese citizens.[1] From this historical perspective, it is perhaps not very surprising that ancient Israelites thought that God wanted them to slaughter the Canaanites. But if God is indeed a God of love, as both the Old and New Testaments teach, we may rightly question whether God ever commanded genocide. Indeed, I think we may rightly refuse to believe that God ever issued such a command. Similarly, I think we may also rightly refuse to believe that God commanded Abraham to sacrifice Isaac and burn him on an altar. Of course, it is quite possible that Abraham *thought* God wanted him to sacrifice Isaac. Abraham lived in a time and place in which human sacrifice occurred with some regularity.

If God is a God of both love and justice, God will not approve of punishments that do not fit the crime or offense. Therefore, God has not approved of the death penalty for adultery, for cursing one's parents, or for breaking the Sabbath. (Punishments such as these conflict even with so stringent a principle as the lex talionis or "eye for an eye" principle; Exod 21:23–24.) When ancient Israelite authors called for such disproportionate punishments, they most likely fell prey to a natural human temptation to announce harsh punishments in hopes of deterring the behavior in question.

But does Jesus himself approve of at least some of these unjust punishments? Recall this passage from the Gospel of Mark:

> Mark 7:9–10 (NIV). "And he [Jesus] said to them, 'You have a fine way of setting aside the commands of God in order to observe your own traditions! For Moses said, *Honor your father and mother*, and, *Anyone who curses their father or mother is to be put to death*.'"

The context of this quotation is a debate with the Pharisees concerning whether giving sufficient funds to the temple absolves one of the duty to support one's aging parents. A big-enough donation does absolve one, according to the Pharisees. Jesus is pointing out that the Pharisees' position here is inconsistent with the

---

1. Gladwell, *Bomber Mafia*, 188–92. In citing these historical facts, I am in no way suggesting that Christians should be pacifists. For a carefully argued defense of just war theory, see Lewis, "Why I Am Not a Pacifist."

Mosaic law which they claim to uphold. So, I think Jesus should be interpreted not as endorsing the death penalty for anyone who curses his parents but simply as insisting on the inconsistency in the Pharisees' position.

Why didn't God simply lay out a list of correct moral rules covering such topics as war, human sacrifice, and criminal punishment?

Is a long list of rules an effective way of getting people to behave morally and to do so for the right reasons? Perhaps there are many things that people need to come to see on their own, through their own experience. Only then will they truly understand that the actions in question are morally right—or wrong—as the case may be. Only then will they do the right thing for the right reasons, not simply because they've been told to do so or because they fear punishment.[2]

But surely God would realize that a book that represents him as commanding genocide is a book that would likely foster misunderstandings about God's nature. I agree. But is God in general concerned to put us in a situation that does not foster misunderstandings? We are dealing here with the general problem of human ignorance, which I take to be part of the problem of evil. There are many things it would be beneficial for us to know that we do not know due to the lack of sufficient evidence and the difficulty of obtaining evidence—for example, cures for many diseases, how to protect ourselves from natural disasters, the right answer to many political questions, whether to marry (or whom to marry), and what career to pursue.

This is not the place to discuss the problem of evil and suffering. But God has apparently decided to "take on" evil and defeat it largely through soft power—for example, preaching, instruction, and various spiritual disciplines. And I think that ignorance is one aspect of the problem of evil and suffering. God expects us to learn to deal with our ignorance by developing virtues such as patience, humility, wisdom, and hope. From this standpoint, is it

---

2. I'm indebted to van Inwagen, "Comments on 'The God of Abraham, Isaac, and Jacob'" (83), for the point that a list of rules is not apt to be an effective motivator.

so surprising that the Bible contains some misleading or confusing content, bearing in mind that God has allowed human authors to speak for him? I don't think so. In any case, the problematic passages are there, so we must read the Bible with discernment.

But in what sense can a book that contains significant moral and theological falsehoods be a message from God? The Bible has authority because it has the approval of Christ—directly in the case of the Old Testament, indirectly (through the apostles and the church) in the case of the New Testament. And thus, the Bible carries with it the presumption of truth. *Simply put, if a given passage is to be regarded as non-authoritative, it must be shown to be such by strong arguments; otherwise, it is authoritative.*

20

Problematic Passages on Moral Issues

NOWADAYS EVERY CHRISTIAN ETHICIST holds that slavery is wrong. But for most of the history of the church, there was no clear understanding of the wrongness of slavery. And this certainly had much to do with biblical passages explicitly teaching about slavery, such as Col 3:22: "Slaves, obey your earthly masters in everything; and do it, not only when their eye is on you and to win their favor, but with sincerity of heart and reverence for the Lord" (NIV). Such passages can readily be used to justify slavery and were often used for that purpose.

The church came into being at a time and in a culture in which slavery was very much part of the socioeconomic structure and generally accepted. (Consider: "During the first century AD, 85 to 90 percent of Rome's population consisted of slaves."[1]) Understandably, there could be no thought of eliminating the practice. An attempt to promote a slave rebellion would certainly have been

---

1. Copan, *Is God a Moral Monster?*, 151.

crushed by the Roman authorities. So, the question was how to live a Christian life within a socioeconomic context involving slavery.

But by the mid-1800s, large numbers of people could see clearly that slavery is contrary to basic principles of love and justice. And so, Christian believers began to see that biblical passages mentioning slavery should not be used to justify it. One lesson to draw, in my judgment, is that *biblical passages touching on specific moral issues always need to be understood and interpreted in the light of the foundational principles of love and justice.* But has the church always taken this approach in interpreting the Bible? I think not. Instead, we find Christians often behaving like lawyers haggling over the wording or meaning of a law, as if this were apt to result in moral insight.

To test a practice under the principle of love, I suggest we need to think primarily in terms of two main factors. First, the harm principle, that is, Is the practice or activity harmful, or does it risk harm or involve intending harm? Harm can of course be of various types: physical, psychological, economic, social (e.g., harm to reputation), and so on. The wrongness of most wrong actions or activities is manifest in terms of the harm principle, for example, murder, rape, stealing, bearing false witness, assault, kidnapping, and adultery. Second, the respect principle: does the practice or activity involve treating a person as having less value than he or she actually has? An example would be spitting in someone's face. This may not cause harm, but it is profoundly disrespectful.

The practice of slavery violates both principles. If I think I can own you and buy or sell you, I am thinking of you as having less value than you really have. I am thinking of you as a commodity. And even if a given practice of slavery is relatively humane, it certainly carries with it the risk of great harm to the slave, including the radical loss of control of one's life and of being forced to devote nearly all of one's time and energy to serving the owner.

These brief reflections on slavery suggest to me that Christians have often misused the Bible in thinking about specific moral issues. Whenever a biblical passage makes a claim about a specific moral issue, that passage needs to be evaluated in terms of the

Problematic Passages on Moral Issues

more basic principles of love and justice. This is not the place for a detailed discussion of specific moral issues, but let me provide four brief illustrations to indicate the types of questions that need to be asked.

Consider the conclusion James (the brother of Jesus) draws in one of the early controversies of the church (on circumcision):

> Acts 15:19–21 (NRSV). "I have reached the decision that we should not trouble those Gentiles who are turning to God, but we should write to them to abstain only from things polluted by idols and from fornication and from *whatever has been strangled and from blood*. For in every city, for generations past, Moses has had those who proclaim him, for he has been read aloud every sabbath in the synagogues" (italics added).

James's decision seems a bit odd in context because the apostle Peter has just said (Acts 15:10 NRSV), "Why are you putting God to the test by placing on the neck of the disciples a yoke that neither our ancestors nor we have been able to bear?" And the council (James included) agrees that gentiles need not be circumcised. Yet James insists on rules about eating blood. Is he thinking of verses such as Deut 12:23 (NRSV): "Only be sure you do not eat the blood; for the blood is the life, and you shall not eat the life with the meat"? Perhaps not. James may be thinking that the rule about eating blood was given *prior to* the laws that were laid down during the trek to the promised land. And so, that rule applies to everyone, Jew and Gentile alike. After all, James no doubt assumed that Moses wrote Genesis, and in Gen 9:4 we read, "You must not eat meat that has its lifeblood still in it" (NIV).

Today, many people eat blood sausage (which has a lot of blood in it), and the Maasai in Africa drink a mixture of blood and milk. Does anyone want to make a moral issue of such things today? (Of course, there are plenty of vegetarians and vegans, but the issue for them is not about eating blood *in particular*.) I have suggested that we need to ask two questions: Does eating blood harm anyone?[2] Does it disrespect anyone? If the answers are

---

2. If harm to animals is to be considered, it will of course lead to much

Is the Bible the Word of God?

negative—as I believe they are, then the Old Testament rule about eating blood seems quite mysterious. Should Christians insist on ethical rules that apparently have no support from the deeper principles of love and justice? Such an approach to ethics seems very questionable to me.

Consider the following remarks about divorce, attributed to Jesus:

> Mark 10:11 (ESV). "And he [Jesus] said to them, 'Whoever divorces his wife and marries another commits adultery against her, and if she divorces her husband and marries another, she commits adultery.'"

Now, beyond doubt, some people fail to take marriage with sufficient seriousness and justify divorce far too easily. But this passage seems quite severe in its outlook and historically has been used to force people to stay in deeply unhappy marriages. The harm in terms of human misery can be great. For this reason, I submit, the passage needs to be read hyperbolically—as a deliberate exaggeration. It underscores the importance of marriage but should not be applied in a legalistic fashion. And yet, for most of its history, it seems to me, the church interpreted passages on divorce without due regard for the more fundamental principles of love and justice. Divorce was not allowed, except in rare cases.

Let me add that, *taken literally*, Jesus' teaching on divorce is false. By definition, adultery is sexual intercourse between a married person and a person who is not his or her spouse. And a divorced person is no longer married. So, if a divorced person marries someone who is free to marry (e.g., one who is widowed, divorced, or not previously married), their sexual intercourse simply does not count as adultery. And the very fact that Jesus' teaching on divorce is false, *if taken literally*, is a good reason to interpret it figuratively (hyperbolically).

Consider the following instructions about the role of women:

---

more than a prohibition on eating blood. And James certainly was not advocating vegetarianism.

Problematic Passages on Moral Issues

> First Timothy 2:11–14 (ESV). "Let a woman learn quietly with all submissiveness. I do not permit a woman to teach or to exercise authority over a man; rather she is to remain quiet. For Adam was formed first, then Eve; and Adam was not deceived; but the woman was deceived and became a transgressor."

These verses have been, and still are, used to deny women top leadership roles (pastor, priest, bishop) in many Christian denominations. The harm to women is obvious—the denial of important opportunities to use one's talents and abilities. There is also the great loss to the church in terms of leadership. It's not as if there are too many gifted pastors and priests! Once again, the lesson, I submit, is that biblical passages that comment on specific moral issues need to be interpreted in the light of the deeper principles of love and justice.

It has often been suggested that the restrictions on the role of women were needed because of circumstances of the time and place. Maybe. But those "circumstances of time and place" are not referenced in 1 Timothy. Furthermore, conservative theologians rightly observe that the reasons given transcend time and place. Indeed, they do. But do the reasons even make sense? "Adam was created before Eve; therefore, men get to be pastors or priests and women don't." How does that follow? Compare: "Older brothers are created before their younger brothers, so older brothers can be pastors, but their younger brothers cannot." No one would endorse such an argument. And is there any hint in Gen 3 that Adam is somehow less at fault than Eve? Didn't both Adam and Eve offer rationalizations for their disobedience? And don't we deceive ourselves when we rationalize? The argument in 1 Timothy simply doesn't add up.

A last illustration concerns same-sex unions or marriages. Let me first note that in my view, many sexual practices, whether heterosexual or homosexual, can readily be seen as morally problematic because of the harm principle, for example, prostitution, sexual relations between adults and minors, and promiscuity. I am focusing here on the specific issue of committed unions between same-sex partners. I doubt that Saint Paul had any such unions in mind when he wrote about homosexuality. Be that as it may, where is the harm or risk of harm in committed same-sex relationships (beyond the risks involved in any marriage)? As far as I can see, the harm principle does not apply in such cases. Does same-sex marriage somehow inherently involve disrespect of one partner for another? Plainly, it does not. Many would point out that same-sex couples cannot produce children. But neither can heterosexual couples who are infertile. So, that point settles nothing—marriage doesn't have to be for the purpose of procreation.

My general observation is this: wherever the New Testament comments on specific moral issues, the church has tended to interpret the relevant passages legalistically, when the passages should be understood and interpreted in the light of the more basic principles of love and justice. And I suggest that this underscores the importance of applying the harm and respect principles.

I have been arguing that New Testament passages regarding specific moral issues must be read with careful discernment. (If Jesus read the Old Testament critically, shouldn't we read the New Testament critically?) Whatever message God seeks to communicate through these passages must be consistent with the foundational principles of love and justice. Unfortunately, down through history the church has not interpreted these passages in this way. The assumption that whatever the human author said (or meant) is what God said (or says), has often gone unquestioned. Bluntly stated, faulty hermeneutics has led the church into moral error.

21

The Problem of Hell

AMONG THE MOST IMPORTANT problem passages in the New Testament are those that concern hell. Theologians and philosophers have performed mental gymnastics trying to explain these passages. Here again, I suggest that these passages need to be read with the deeper principles of love and justice in mind.

English translations concerning hell are systematically misleading. In English, "hell" refers to a place of perpetual punishment. That's what the word means. "Gehenna" is the term in the Greek text that is translated as "hell." But Gehenna is *literally* a burning garbage dump near Jerusalem, and so "Gehenna" is a metaphor as used in New Testament passages concerning divine judgment. Accordingly, we must fill in the meaning by looking carefully at what is explicitly said about divine judgment and the afterlife.

A key text regarding hell is in Matthew, chapter 25. The scene is the Day of Judgment, with the Lord separating the "sheep from the goats." The most solemn, disturbing words come right at the end of the chapter:

> Matthew 25:44–46 (NIV). "They also will answer, 'Lord, when did we see you hungry or thirsty or a stranger or needing clothes or sick or in prison, and did not help you?' He will reply, 'I tell you the truth, whatever you did not do for one of the least of these, you did not do for me.' Then they will go away to eternal punishment, but the righteous to eternal life."

Should we understand the passage to be saying that some people will literally be punished forever, without end? Many argue, "Yes, the righteous (or the faithful) will be in heaven forever, *literally*; so, the passage must be understood as saying that the unrighteous (or those who reject God) will be punished forever, *literally*."

But let's think this through with the basic principles of love and justice in mind and on the assumption that God is indeed a God of love and justice. He isn't a God of love sometimes and not others; he's a God of love all the time (or timelessly), right? And he isn't a God of justice sometimes and not others; he's a God of justice all the time (or timelessly), right? I assume a "yes" answer to these questions is correct.

Let's first consider hell from the standpoint of divine love. When we love someone, we care about what is in their long-term best interest. Of course, there is such a thing as "tough" love. Love can be firm and uncompromising. But it remains focused on what's best for the one loved. Can it be in anyone's best interest to be punished forever? I don't see how, assuming "punishment" is taken literally. And if we take "eternal" literally, we surely must take "punishment" literally, too. In fact, the punishment involves being placed in an "eternal fire" (v. 41). Is "eternal fire" to be taken literally also? If "eternal" must be taken literally, should "fire" be taken literally too? Be that as it may, even if "eternal fire" is a metaphor, it plainly indicates something awful, something very painful spiritually if not physically—*the spiritual equivalent of being thrown into an everlasting fire*. Would it not be better to simply cease to exist, rather than to be made to suffer such pain *forever*? I think so, and I think most people would agree with me.

Now let's consider hell from the standpoint of divine justice. One classic attempt to defend the doctrine of hell goes like this: "God is not only loving, but also just. As a just God, he must punish sin fully. And those who have rejected God, have committed the greatest offense possible. Offending an infinite God merits infinite punishment. And that's what hell is."

The mental gymnastics here are dramatic. Should we be convinced? When we say that God is infinite, we mean roughly that he is unlimited in power and knowledge. How do we get from "God is unlimited in power and knowledge" to "those who offend God merit literally everlasting punishment"? The logical linkage isn't even close to being clear.

Moreover, the seriousness of an offense is at least in part a function of the harm done. Can humans harm almighty God? Arguably, yes. If one harms a child, one simultaneously harms his (or her) parents, right? If so, then by analogy, if one harms a person, one harms his (or her) Creator. But here's the crucial point: no human can send God to eternal hell. No one can do that much harm to God. Nor can one human send another human to hell. One human can tempt another human to sin, but no one will be in hell unless God puts him there. So, how can the fitting punishment for a sin (or sins) be eternal hell? That would be a violation of even so harsh a principle as the lex talionis ("an eye for an eye").

But we need to step back and consider the more basic claim that a just God must punish sin fully. This claim apparently presupposes that justice is a matter of "evening the score" or paying the offender back "in kind." ("Anyone who maims another shall suffer the same injury in return: fracture for fracture, eye for eye, tooth for tooth. The injury inflicted is the injury to be suffered"— Lev 24:19–20 NRSV.) But that presupposition is by no means self-evident. For one thing, taken straightforwardly, it involves maiming maimers, torturing torturers, raping rapists, blinding those who blind others, and so on. That indicates, I think, that there is something morally warped about this idea. Moreover, as previously noted, Jesus apparently denies the lex talionis in his Sermon on the Mount. Finally, if God is required to give people exactly what they deserve, God cannot be gracious, since grace is *unmerited or undeserved* favor.

Without the lex talionis, I see no good reason to suppose that divine love and justice ever come into conflict. And if they do not conflict, then divine punishment would presumably be analogous to the punishment a child may receive from a loving parent. Such punishment is not given "to get even" or "to even the score" but to instruct and to help the child make better choices. But would literally unending punishment (with no chance of escape) help those who suffer it? Even if the inmates of eternal hell happened to learn something—and even if they repented of their sins, it would do them no good; the punishment would go on forever, no matter what.

Philosopher Nicholas Wolterstorff argues that justice involves treating people in accord with their worth. We are unjust when we demean people, that is, treat them as having less value than they actually have. From this perspective, love and justice do not conflict. To the extent that we genuinely love a person (care about her), we will not demean her.[1]

But what about people who don't love God and don't want to be in heaven with him? Don't they have to be eternally punished, separated from God forever? No, God has options. God creates people and he can "uncreate" them—cause them to stop existing. God could also give second chances, if he wanted to.

Some have argued that eternal punishment is just because those in hell continue to sin. We might call this the whack-a-mole view of hell. Each time a person in hell sins, God provides the appropriate (deserved) punishment. Sin-whack, sin-whack, sin-whack, and so on, forever. There are at least two problems with this view of hell. First, this view has God playing an endless game of whack-a-mole with the damned. To what end? Simply retribution, payback, going on forever. Is such an end worth pursuing? I think not, especially since God has the option of letting the damned cease to exist. Second, if those in hell can sin, then they have free will. Only a person who can freely choose evil over good can sin. But if those in hell have free will, then they can choose the good.

---

1. Wolterstorff, *Justice in Love*, 93.

They can repent. If they repent, why would God keep them in hell? That would hardly be loving. So, by implication, hell is escapable on this view. Thus, the whack-a-mole view is not a defense of the traditional view after all.

In his novel *The Great Divorce*, C. S. Lewis explored the idea of an escapable hell. Those in hell can escape it (and gain heaven) through genuine repentance.[2] This version of hell has the advantage that the punishment is not retributive. God isn't "paying back" those who reject divine love; their suffering is meant to instruct and help them. Still, in this version, some, and perhaps a great many, will never repent and so will be in hell forever.[3] From the standpoint of divine love, wouldn't there be a point at which annihilation would be an act of mercy? The sinner just isn't going to repent. Also, if God knew (from all eternity) who these unrepentant sinners would be, why did he create them? It hardly seems an act of love to create a person knowing in advance (or timelessly) that he or she would wind up miserable in hell forever.

The traditional view faces this same problem, on the assumption that God creates people knowing how they'd wind up. Is it an act of love to create someone knowing that he or she would be punished forever in hell? In fact, it seems cruel. Wouldn't it be better not

---

2. Since *The Great Divorce* is a novel and not a work of systematic theology, I do not assume that Lewis held the view of hell he explores in that book. Defenders of the traditional view would appeal to the story of the rich man and Lazarus to deny that hell is escapable (once the punishment starts): "Between us and you a great chasm has been fixed, so that those who want to go from here to you cannot, nor can anyone cross over from there to us" (Luke 16:26 NIV). But the story is arguably a parable and, if so, not intended as a literal account of the situation of the damned.

3. In one passage in *The Great Divorce*, George Macdonald, the guide, says, "You can repent and come out of it again. But there may come a time when you can do that no longer. Then there will be no you left. . . ." Lewis, *Great Divorce*, 75. Is Lewis suggesting that at some point the unrepentant simply cease to exist? The answer is not made entirely clear, as far as I can see. But if the unrepentant are annihilated after being allowed ample time to repent, the Great Divorce view of hell would seem defensible, but it departs from the traditional view in two important ways: (1) the damned can escape hell by repenting and (2) the unrepentant are not punished forever.

to exist at all than to wind up being miserable forever in hell? I think so, and again, I think most people would agree with me.[4]

Here is another consideration in support of a non-literal interpretation of "eternal punishment." In the book of Revelation, we read:

> Revelation 14:9–11 (NIV). "If anyone worships the beast . . . he will be tormented with *burning sulfur* in the presence of the holy angels and of the Lamb. And the *smoke* of their torment rises *forever and ever*. There is no rest, *day or night* for those who worship the beast . . ." (italics added).

This sounds like support for the traditional view of hell, right? But wait. The author of Revelation plainly knew the Old Testament well, and he is here alluding to a passage in Isaiah:

> Isaiah 34:9–10 (NIV). "Edom's streams will be turned into pitch, her dust into *burning sulfur*; her land will become blazing pitch! It will not be quenched *night or day*; its *smoke* will rise *forever*" (italics added).

The parallel phrasing is obvious. But ancient Edom was in a specific geographical location (now in southwestern Jordan). Edom had been Israel's constant enemy and was due for punishment. But was the punishment literally eternal? Is the smoke of destruction still rising? Clearly not. (And surely no country on this planet will be on fire forever, literally speaking.) Thus, "forever" in the Isaiah passage is used hyperbolically. But if "forever" in the Isaiah passage is hyperbolic, then shouldn't "forever and ever" in the Revelation passage also be taken as hyperbolic? A "yes" answer seems at least reasonable.

---

4. Open theists deny that God knows in advance who would be damned (if created) and who would be saved. But even if God does not create people knowing in advance which individuals would be saved and which would be damned, God surely would know in advance that *some* people will reject divine love. If that's correct, then eternal hell is a problem for open theists too. For God creates knowing that some people will be miserable in hell forever (even if God does not know who they are in advance).

Perhaps here it should also be noted that Jesus often used hyperbole. "If your right eye causes you to sin, tear it out and throw it away" (Matt 5:29 NRSV). "When you give alms, do not let your left hand know what your right hand is doing" (Matt 6:3 NRSV). "If you have faith the size of a mustard seed, you will say to this mountain, 'Move from here to there,' and it will move; and nothing will be impossible for you" (Matt 17:20–21 NRSV). Might Jesus have employed hyperbole in speaking of the last judgment? I think that possibility should be kept in mind.

But if the righteous have literally eternal life, the unrighteous must have literally eternal punishment, right? Not so fast.

First, a small point, but perhaps worth noting. The Greek word translated "eternal" is *aiōnion*. But this word isn't always translated as *eternal*. For example, in Rom 16:25, Paul speaks of "the mystery hidden for long ages (*aiōniois*) past" (NIV). So, even when the word is used literally, the meaning isn't always and necessarily "eternal."

Second, the image of hellfire suggests total destruction. What happens when a log is thrown into the fire? It is consumed. Burnt up. Destroyed.

Third, if we are willing to consider non-literal interpretations of "eternal," might we take "eternal" to have the force of "once and for all"?[5] In other words, perhaps the language of eternal punishment is meant to indicate the *finality* of divine judgment. There won't be a second chance. Is that interpretation possible? Plausible? Plausible enough to create doubt about the traditional claim that hell is literally eternal? I suggest that it is.

Fourth, I think we should be wary of resting our belief in eternal life on the meaning of one Greek word. According to Christian theology, God has gone to great lengths to save humans and to give them the best life possible after death. So, why would God end that wonderful post-death life after five hours? Five days? Five years? Five hundred years? What sense would it make for a God of love to annihilate those enjoying heavenly bliss? In short,

---

5. Second Thessalonians 1:9 speaks of "eternal destruction." Could that mean destroyed, *once and for all*?

our belief in literally eternal life depends not on the meaning of one Greek word but on the logic of love.

Here, I believe, is a crucial point. *Those who insist on the doctrine of literally everlasting punishment are in effect pitting their approach to interpretation against the underlying biblical principles of love and justice.* Doesn't the apparent impossibility of reconciling the traditional doctrine of hell with the principles of love and justice provide good grounds for doubt about that approach to interpretation? I think it does. If so, we might at least conclude that we can't be sure about the fate of those (if any) who reject the love of God.

One last thought. The problem of evil and suffering is usually thought to be the strongest objection to the belief in an almighty God of love. But if we posit literally everlasting suffering in hell, we create an arguably worse problem for Christian theism. At least the suffering in this present life will one day come to an end. It ends at death for each of us. But the suffering of eternal hell is suffering that never ends. Never. On this view, the world ends in a radical divide between heaven and hell, with both going on forever in an unresolved dualism of good and evil—a dualism of those blessed forever and those who suffer forever. (The strangeness of this dualism may be underscored by asking these questions: "Could those blessed with eternal life enjoy their beatitude fully if they know a loved one is suffering in eternal hell? Isn't the happiness of those who love linked to the state or situation of their loved ones?") The crucial point is this: the doctrine of eternal hell adds infinite, unrelieved, unresolved suffering to the problem of evil and suffering, making the problem far worse.

22

Epilogue

CHRISTIANS USE THE BIBLE as support for their theological and moral views. But they often do this without asking the fundamental question "why think the Bible is authoritative?" Too often Christians simply assume the Bible is inspired or authoritative, without any justification. And when the question of biblical authority is asked, it is often given answers that do not hold up under scrutiny.

I have written in the conviction that seriously confronting the question of biblical authority has dramatic implications. It forces us to deal honestly with the numerous problem passages in the Bible, which range from apparent factual errors, to apparent failed prophecies, to morally and theologically troubling statements or narratives. It forces us to abandon simplistic approaches to interpreting the Bible. I think it forces us to see that a defense of biblical authority involves multiple premises, which may be defensible but are by no means certain. Finally, in my opinion, it forces us to admit that the Bible is by no means an inerrant or infallible document. If the Bible is an authority, in my view, it is a fallible

Is the Bible the Word of God?

authority. That said, I've repeatedly stressed that most of what we humans know we have learned from fallible authorities.

I have argued that, from a Christian perspective, the authority of the Bible traces back to the authority of Jesus Christ. His authority is based on his character, his actions, his teaching, his miracles, and his resurrection. To the extent that his life, actions, and teachings plausibly fulfill Old Testament prophecies, his authority is further supported. Of course, all this raises the question, "How do we know about the life and teachings of Jesus Christ?"

I have outlined arguments for regarding the Synoptic Gospels as historically reliable. These arguments presuppose the existence of God. Those who deny the existence of God are virtually bound to find the accounts of miracles in the gospels (literally) incredible. But those who believe in God should approach the miracle-accounts in the gospels with an open mind. In addition, many agnostics may find the miracle-accounts in the gospels hard to dismiss as superstition or fabrication.

I have also explained why I find unconvincing other reasons often given for dismissing the gospel accounts as unreliable. For example, the hermeneutic of suspicion is an approach to interpretation that fails to give historical documents the benefit of the doubt. And the claim that the gospels are replete with contradictions is a gross exaggeration in my estimation. Furthermore, the claim that we don't know the original content of the gospels because of massive copying errors is a claim which simply does not hold up in the light of the evidence.

So, how do we know about the life and teachings of Jesus? Primarily by reading the gospels as historical documents. And we can do this without assuming that the gospels are divinely inspired or divinely approved.

From the gospels we learn that Jesus was a genuine prophet. He has authority by virtue of his exemplary life, his insightful teaching, his miracles, his death, and resurrection. Also, from the gospels we learn that the apostles underwent a long period of instruction from Jesus himself. In addition, from the book of Acts (and some New Testament epistles), we learn that the apostles put

Epilogue

what they learned from Jesus into practice. Through their preaching and teaching, the church came into being and grew rapidly in numbers. The apostles nurtured the church as it grew.

The apostles have authority because they underwent a long period of instruction from Jesus and because they put that instruction into practice by bringing the church into being and nurturing it as it grew. The New Testament has authority insofar as it accurately reflects the teaching of the apostles. And the church selected the books of the New Testament with a view to identifying writings that accurately reflect apostolic teaching.

How about the Old Testament? From a Christian point of view, the authority of Scripture ultimately derives from the authority of Christ. And as we have seen, Jesus Christ regarded the Old Testament as an important theological and moral authority. Naturally enough, Christians follow Christ in regarding the Old Testament as authoritative.

None of the above claims support the idea that the Bible is inerrant or infallible. And a defense of the authority of the Bible must address the presence of the problematic passages in it. I have discussed many of the most problematic passages, and for reasons I've given, I see no credible defense of the claim that the Bible is inerrant or infallible. The Bible is a fallible authority.

Accordingly, the Bible must be read with discernment. It is not enough to determine what the original human authors said (or meant)—even when we can do that. As we read the Bible we must constantly ask, "What does God want us to learn from this book, this passage, or this verse?" Most importantly, passages that apparently conflict with the fundamental Christian teachings about love and justice (including the love and justice of God) must either be regarded as erroneous or else interpreted in such a way as to be consistent with love and justice. I have tried to illustrate this discerning approach to interpretation in my discussion of morally problematic passages of the Bible, including passages concerning hell.

In the present theological and political climate, my view of biblical authority and my defense of it will undoubtedly be rejected by many, and indeed, viewed as pernicious. To those who view my arguments in this negative way, I pose the following questions. First, where exactly has my reasoning gone wrong? Can you spell this out without making very implausible claims? Second, what is your own defense of the authority of the Bible? If you have no defense, do you think none is needed?

In our current intellectual environment, fueled as it is by the internet, social media, and divisive politics, overconfidence seems to be the order of the day. Too often reasoning is used minimally: short retorts and ad hominem arguments carry the day. What seems to matter is belonging to the "right tribe," the group of people who share the values and opinions of the arguer. In this work, I hope I've displayed a different use of logic and reasoning. One that seeks an overall account that makes sense, avoids falling into manifest implausibility, and one that follows the arguments "wherever they go." Have I succeeded? No doubt the reader will be the judge!

Appendix

In Vitro Fertilization and the Right to Life

ACCORDING TO A DECISION by the Supreme Court of the State of Alabama, embryos (fertilized eggs) created outside of the uterus are children—extra-uterine persons.[1] This decision certainly invites a closer look at questions about the right to life.

The main argument of the Alabama Court is that unborn children are nevertheless children. And where a child is located—inside or outside a uterus—is irrelevant.[2] My interest is not in whether the *legal* reasoning of the Alabama Court is correct but in deeper philosophical principles that come into play in thinking about in vitro fertilization. From this perspective, even if the Alabama Court's decision is correct from the standpoint of Alabama state law, it is unjustified from a moral point of view.

The following principles are commonly employed in debates about the right to life: (a) human life begins at conception, and

---

1. *LePage v. Mobile Infirmary Clinic, Inc.* In 2024 Alabama's Supreme Court ruled that frozen embryos are children and that anyone who destroys them may be liable for wrongful death.
2. *LePage v Mobile Infirmary Clinic, Inc.*, 2, 17.

APPENDIX

(b) murder is the intentional and unjustified termination of a human life.[3] I argue that principle (b)—call it the *human-life principle*—is, as usually understood, deeply flawed. And I propose an alternative.[4]

GROUNDING THE RIGHT TO LIFE

What grounds the right to life? This is not an easy question to answer. On the traditional Christian view, humans are created in the image of God, and this is what gives them their special moral status, a status that is higher than that of other living things, such as plants and non-human animals.[5] But what does it mean to be in the image of God? Presumably, it means that humans resemble God in some way. What way? Theologians differ on this issue. But surely, being similar to God involves rather exalted capacities, such as having free will, being able to think and act morally, and being able to love (i.e., to care about others).

Of course, normal adult humans have these exalted capacities. The problem is that many humans apparently lack these capacities, for example, the severely mentally impaired, those with dementia, the permanently comatose, very young children, infants, and the developing fetus.[6] (Here I am counting human fetuses as human beings; I'll consider a question about that momentarily.)

One response to this problem is, so to speak, to lower the bar—that is, to hold that the qualities or capacities that ground the right to life are much less exalted. For example, perhaps being merely a subject of conscious mental states—such as desires, pains,

---

3. For a much-anthologized example of reasoning based on principles of this sort, see Noonan, "Abortion Is Not Morally Permissible," 789–96.

4. The issue in the Alabama case is wrongful killing rather than murder. But my interest is in familiar, general principles that might be thought to apply to the case of in vitro fertilization.

5. "Whoever sheds the blood of a human, by a human shall that person's blood be shed; for in his own image God made humankind" (Gen 9:6 NRSV).

6. The difficulty of grounding human rights on capacities is well articulated by Wolterstorff, *Justice: Rights and Wrongs*, 329–33.

and pleasures—is enough to ground the right to life. The trouble with this idea is that many non-human animals, such as dogs, cats, chimps, and dolphins, have these less exalted capacities. And so, this idea leads to a right to life that extends to many animals and puts them on a par with humans.

Another response is to claim that *simply being human* grounds the right to life. But what does "simply being human" mean? Apparently, it just means "belonging to the species *Homo sapiens.*" And why does belonging to this species confer a moral status not accorded to other species, such as *Canis lupus* or *Pan troglodytes*?

Suppose someone were to argue like this: "Using a microscope, we have examined the DNA of the species *Canis lupus* and have determined that this species has a moral status higher than that of *Homo sapiens*. The life of a member of *Canis lupus* is of greater value than the life of a member of *Homo sapiens*." I think the proper response would be this: "There is no way you could have done this. The value of a life, from a moral point of view, cannot be determined by some *merely* biological feature. Unless a biological feature correlates with some clearly morally relevant feature, such as the ability to feel pain or to think about right and wrong, the biological feature has no bearing on the value of life."

We reject racism because it involves regarding some morally irrelevant feature, such as skin color, as determinative of one's moral status relative to others. But mere species differences (apart from any correlation with clearly morally relevant properties) are not morally relevant differences. On analogy with racism, the appeal to *mere* species membership is "speciesism."[7]

THREE PRINCIPLES

The human-life principle might be understood in at least three different ways. Perhaps the most natural (and common) understanding is this:

---

7. The philosopher best known for stressing the moral problem of *speciesism* is Peter Singer. See Singer, *Practical Ethics*, 48–54.

Appendix

1. Murder is the intentional and unjustified termination of the life of a human being.

But as we've just seen, the right to life is not plausibly grounded on mere species membership. And a human being is a member of the species *Homo sapiens*. So, this principle seems to put the rule against murder on a false footing. That's the main problem with it.

But let's also note a special problem that arises if we try to apply (1) to the case of in vitro fertilization. No one doubts that a zygote which is formed when a man and woman have sex is a human zygote as opposed to, say, a chimp or wolf zygote. The fetus is a developing *human* organism. (From here on, I'll use "fetus" to refer to the developing human organism from fertilization to birth.) But is the fetus a human *being* from "day one"? That is doubtful. To claim that a zygote is a human being is on a par with claiming that an acorn is an oak tree.[8] *An acorn simply is not an oak tree and that's that.* We must avoid the error of regarding an organism in the very early stages of its development as if it were a fully developed member of the species in question. I'll refer to this as the acorn-oak issue.

If I toss an acorn into the fireplace, is my act equivalent to setting a full-grown oak tree on fire? I think not, and I think most people would agree. The one act is surely more momentous than the other. (I am not claiming that one act is right, and one is wrong, just that they differ in significance.)

Consider this. Many of those strongly opposed to abortion allow for it in the case of pregnancy through rape. But they would insist that the abortion occur as soon as possible in the pregnancy. Waiting till, say, month seven or eight of the pregnancy would be seen as wrong. But this suggests that even those who strongly oppose abortion tend to regard the moral status of the zygote or embryo as different (and lower) than that of a child or human adult.

So, principle (1) does not provide a compelling philosophical ground for the claim that killing innocent human beings is wrong, nor does it clearly apply in the case of embryos.

---

8. The acorn-oak tree analogy is borrowed from Thomson, "Defense of Abortion," 863.

Should we understand the human-life principle this way?

> 2. Murder is the intentional and unjustified termination of any organism belonging to *Homo sapiens*. ("Any organism" includes zygotes, embryos, and fetuses.)

Unlike principle (1), this principle clearly applies in the case of in vitro fertilization. But like principle (1), it apparently presupposes that mere biological classification is what grounds the right to life. And we've already seen that this is not true.

Consider a third version of the human-life principle:

> 3. Murder is the intentional and unjustified killing of a human *person*.

This definition invites the question "what is a person?" We often use the term "person" as interchangeable with "human being." But philosophers and theologians have frequently used the word "person" to refer to entities capable of thinking, knowing, and moral agency. For example, God and angels count as persons in this sense, according to traditional Christian theology. So, given this understanding of "person," definition (3) has the advantage of moving us beyond mere biological classification. It locates the value of life in something close to (or identical with) the image of God idea. This makes principle (3) radically different than the first two principles.

But if "person" means "entity capable of knowing and moral agency," then terminating a zygote or embryo would apparently not count as murder, given definition (3). A zygote or embryo surely does not have the capacity to know or to act morally.

The third definition, however, may seem to imply that killing even a newborn baby is not murder and that killing a permanently comatose human is not murder. If the third definition has these implications, it is certainly problematic. I'll return to this issue momentarily.

Notice three things. First, these three definitions have different implications—differing implications that matter. Second, two of them put the principle concerning murder on a false, merely biological basis. Third, to propose or defend any of these definitions

APPENDIX

is to make a *philosophical* proposal. None of these definitions is self-evidently correct.

THE SOUL THEORY

An old idea in the Christian tradition is that the value of human life depends on the possession of a soul. From this perspective, each human being has both a physical body and a non-physical soul. And the soul is the part of us that has the capacity to think, to reason, to know, to understand right and wrong, and to make choices.

Might the soul ground the right to life? Philosopher Paul Herrick invites us to consider that possibility:

> Suppose that each person is an immaterial soul temporarily animating a physical body. [. . . .] Suppose further that the absolute value of an individual is rooted *not* in that person's body . . . , but in that person's immaterial soul, understood as a creation of God and the basis of the human potential to reason, act freely, and exercise moral autonomy—whether those capacities are expressed, temporarily lost, or yet to be expressed.[9]

I want to underscore a crucial part of this quotation. Note that Herrick speaks of capacities that may be temporarily lost or yet to be expressed. Think of a person who is under a general anesthetic for the purpose of heart surgery. Such a person is temporarily unable to exercise his mental capacities to think, reason, make choices, and so on. But the capacities have not vanished; rather, they've been temporarily blocked. The patient will (if all goes well) be able to exercise his mental capacities upon awakening. Similarly, a person in a temporary coma will (or at least may) regain full use of her mental capacities upon awakening. With these examples in mind, if and when a fetus has a soul, it would have *capacities* it is not yet able to exercise, such as the capacity to reason and to act freely.

In contrast to cases in which capacities are temporarily blocked, when "brain death" occurs, all electrical activity in the

---

9. Herrick, *Philosophy, Reasoned Belief, and Faith*, 342.

In Vitro Fertilization and the Right to Life

brain has ceased. Nowadays a brain-dead person is considered dead, period. For those who believe each human has a soul, brain death would signal the separation of the soul from the body.

What has this got to do with in vitro fertilization? Well, assuming each human has a soul, when does he or she possess it?

Start here. Our conscious mental activity depends on the functioning of our brains. Thus, a brain injury can temporarily or even permanently block our capacity to think, reason, make choices, and so on. Similarly, too much alcohol can partially or even completely block our mental functioning, but that's because alcohol affects the functioning of the brain (e.g., by killing brain cells).

Other parts of our bodies do not seem to have a *direct* effect on our mental capacities. When they do influence our mental capacities, it is because of their effect on the functioning of the brain. I might have an arm or leg amputated and still be able to reason, to think about right and wrong, and to make choices. Of course, I might become depressed by the loss of a limb, but I won't be depressed if my brain isn't functioning. And a heart attack might block my capacity to reason or to think clearly, but that's because it affects the flow of blood to my brain.

The upshot is this: assuming humans have a soul, it apparently links to the body at the brain. Accordingly, if we humans have souls, we don't have them until we have a brain. When do we have a brain? Well, like everything else in fetal development, the brain develops gradually. It doesn't appear fully formed all at once. So, the acorn-oak issue reappears.

But, for present purposes, I think one fact is crucial: electrical activity begins in the brain at about the eighth week of pregnancy: "By week 8, electrical activity begins in the brain."[10] (Week eight of the pregnancy is, oddly, six weeks from conception, as the medical community measures the time of pregnancy.[11]) Thus, "it is not

---

10. De Bellafonds, "When Does Your Baby Develop a Brain?"

11. "When a sperm fertilizes an egg, a person is already officially two weeks pregnant. As nonsensical as that sounds, it's the simplest way medical professionals can date a pregnancy." Sanders, "5 Misunderstandings of Pregnancy Biology."

until around week six [from fertilization] that the first electrical brain activity begins to occur."[12] Prior to that time, the developing structures would seem *relevantly* analogous to the situation of brain death: *no electrical activity is present*. Accordingly, it is implausible to suggest that the soul-brain linkage is in place prior to week eight of the pregnancy. (I am not claiming that the soul-brain linkage occurs at week eight of the pregnancy, only that it is very implausible to suppose the linkage occurs prior to that time.)

The upshot for in vitro fertilization is this: whatever value an extra-uterine embryo may have, it is not the same as that of a child, who has both body and soul. The soul grounds the special value of human life.

Note: nothing I've said implies that zygotes and embryos are without value. Nothing I've said suggests that it is morally permissible to treat them as one wishes. But the ground of their value is different than the value of a human being who has both soul and body. (I'll return to this issue momentarily.)

MORE ON THE SOUL THEORY

How does the soul become linked to the body? Theologians have offered two main theories about this. On one theory, called *creationism*, for each individual human, God creates a soul and links it to the fetus by divine decree. On this view, each linkage between a soul and body is a miracle. According to the other theory, called *traducianism*, God has set up natural processes so that body and soul are both produced via sexual reproduction. For example, one might think that when a fetal brain develops to a certain point, it automatically generates a soul. (On this view, the miracle is in the way God set things up originally, not in each individual case.)

Can we specify precisely when the soul is linked to the body? I see no way to do that. I have indicated why I think it would be implausible to suppose that the linkage occurs prior to week eight

---

12. Gordon, "Everything You Need to Know."

In Vitro Fertilization and the Right to Life

of the pregnancy. Is there a point at which, assuming humans have souls, the fetus very likely has one? Perhaps. Consider:

> The experience of pain starts with the senses detecting something noxious. Those signals then have to travel to the cortex, the outer layer of the brain that helps interpret that sensation [signal]. In human fetuses, those brain connections don't exist until about week 24 or 25 of pregnancy.[13]

Similarly, the Royal College of Obstetricians and Gynecologists reports as follows:

> . . . the cortex is necessary for pain perception, [and] . . . connections from the periphery to the cortex are not intact before 24 weeks of gestation, . . . [therefore] it is . . . reasonable to conclude that a fetus cannot experience pain in any sense prior to this gestation.[14]

These facts about brain connections do not prove that the fetus feels pain at twenty-four or twenty-five weeks. There's no way to know for sure when a fetus can *feel* pain. But it seems to me that, if the necessary brain connections are in place, then it's likely the fetus can feel pain. And the felt quality of pain is a mental state, occurring in the soul, if we humans have souls. So, I suggest that it is likely the soul is present at about week twenty-four or twenty-five—if not before. And once the fetus has a soul, it has a right to life, even though many capacities of the soul are yet to be exercised.[15]

---

13. Sanders, "5 Misunderstandings of Pregnancy Biology."
14. Royal College of Obstetricians and Gynecologists, "Fetal Awareness."
15. Here it may be of interest to note that when *Roe v. Wade* (1973) became law, fetal viability—the time when the fetus can survive outside the womb—was about twenty-eight weeks. Currently fetal viability is at twenty-three or twenty-four weeks because of advances in medical technology. Under *Roe v. Wade*, states were not allowed to ban abortion prior to viability. For a brief discussion of viability as a morally significant point in pregnancy, see Singer, *Practical Ethics*, 108–10.

Appendix

POTENTIAL

The soul theory does not imply that zygotes and embryos are without value. Even if they do not have souls, they may yet have an important moral status, by virtue of their potential.

In this context, to say that a zygote or embryo has potential is roughly to say that, if properly nurtured, it probably will—or at least may well—develop into a baby (or into a fetus) that has a soul.

How do we assess the value of such a potential? This seems to me a very difficult question. Here are five things to consider:

1. The acorn-oak example suggests, I think, that *being potentially X* is of less value than simply *being X*. An acorn is potentially an oak tree, but I think most of us regard a full-grown oak tree (in normal circumstances) as of greater value than an acorn. That's why tossing an acorn into the fireplace is less momentous than burning down a full-grown oak tree.

2. Even in normal pregnancies, "up to 50 percent of fertilized eggs do not implant in the uterus, researchers have estimated."[16] Now, if a fertilized egg is a child, does it seem odd that almighty God would have set up natural processes with relatively high rates of non-implantation? It seems very odd to me. Might it be that fertilized eggs do not have a high intrinsic value but are a means, which God *often but by no means always* uses, to an end—the creation of a human person?

3. Consider an egg-sperm pair shortly *before* they've joined together. What is the potential of that pair? It would seem to be the same as that of a zygote, or nearly the same. But most of us would not consider it wrong to prevent that pair from joining, e.g., by use of a spermicidal foam, even though, in doing so, we destroy or eliminate an important potential.[17]

---

16. Sanders, "5 Misunderstandings of Pregnancy Biology."

17. I recognize, of course, that some do regard the use of such contraceptive methods as wrong.

In Vitro Fertilization and the Right to Life

4. Extra-uterine embryos have value. To break into a clinic that stores them and wantonly destroy them would be wrong. But is their value intrinsic or instrumental? Surely part of their value consists in the fact that they are a means to the creation of a baby (or human person). Do they also have *intrinsic* value, i.e., value if they remain frozen and are never used to make a woman pregnant? I am unsure. Interestingly, one of the plaintiffs in *LePage v. Mobile Infirmary Clinic, Inc.* specified that any *unused* frozen embryos should be discarded after five years. Another plaintiff specified that any *unused* frozen embryos should be donated for research (in which case they would be destroyed eventually).[18] Personally, I am unable to find fault with these stipulations.

5. What about the case of a zygote (more technically, a blastocyst) implanted in the uterus? Here the zygote's potential to develop into a baby has a good chance of being realized. Three comments: (a) Terminating the zygote (or blastocyst) would not be murder according to definition (3) above—a definition that I think is on the right track. (b) Only humans with a soul have a right to life, which is grounded in the exalted capacities the soul possesses. And, as I've argued, zygotes, blastocysts, and embryos do not have a soul. (c) The decision to terminate is momentous because of the potentially valuable future of the zygote (or blastocyst). But this does not mean that terminating the zygote (or blastocyst) is murder. (Note: It can be wrong to kill a person even if they don't have a valuable future, as may arguably be the situation in some cases, e.g., a person with severe dementia. Such a person would still have the right to life because he or she has a soul.)

Plainly, the philosophical issue of the value of (and treatment of) potentials is complex and tricky. No doubt this is an area in which opinions differ widely.

And we must not impose our moral views on others, via legislation, unless we have very strong arguments to advance, as

---

18. *LePage v. Mobile Infirmary Clinic, Inc.*, 24.

the abolitionists did in the case of slavery. But I see little hope of locating arguments regarding the treatment of potentials that have anywhere near the force of the arguments against slavery. So, I think the value and treatment of potentials (as regards discarding them, donating them for research, or terminating them) is best left as an area in which individuals may freely follow the dictates of their consciences.

The soul theory I've outlined is plainly speculative, although it does employ some ideas that are at home in the Christian tradition. But if the theory, as I've elaborated it, is reasonable, then I think it exposes weaknesses in much of the contemporary discussion of right-to-life issues.

In closing, let me simply emphasize that, currently, deeply flawed principles are front and center in the debates about the right to life. These principles do not provide solid grounds for making laws. Laws must be based on strong and defensible arguments, not on arguments that can readily be seen to be flawed. And while the soul theory is just a theory, I think elaborating it helps us see weaknesses in the currently popular arguments about the right to life.

Works Cited

Abraham, William J. *Crossing the Threshold of Divine Revelation.* Grand Rapids: Eerdmans, 2006.

Adams, Robert Merrihew. *Finite and Infinite Goods: A Framework for Ethics.* Oxford: Oxford University Press, 1999.

Augustine (Saint). *De Doctrina Christiana.* http://www.ntslibrary.com/PDF%20 Books/Augustine%20doctrine.pdf.

Blomberg, Craig L. *The Historical Reliability of the Gospels.* 2nd ed. Downers Grove, IL: IVP Academic, 2007.

Boyd, Craig A., and Raymond J. VanArragon, "Ethics Is Based on Natural Law." In *Contemporary Debates in Philosophy of Religion,* edited by Michael L. Peterson and Raymond J. VanArragon, 299–310. Malden, MA: Blackwell, 2004.

Boyd, Gregory A. "The Open Theism View." In *Divine Foreknowledge: Four Views,* edited by James K. Beilby and Paul R. Eddy, 13–54. Downers Grove, IL: IVP Academic, 2001.

Bruce, F. F. "The Canon of the New Testament." *Theology Matters* 1 (2014) 7–10.

———. *The Canon of Scripture.* Downers Grove, IL: IVP Academic, 1988.

———. *The New Testament Documents: Are They Reliable?* Downers Grove, IL: IVP, 1971.

Caesar, Gaius Julius. *Caesar's Gallic War.* Translated by Joseph Pearl. Great Neck, NY: Barron's Educational Series, 1962.

Copan, Paul. *Is God a Moral Monster?: Making Sense of the Old Testament God.* Grand Rapids: Baker, 2011.

Curley, Edwin. "Reply to Van Inwagen." In *Divine Evil: The Moral Character of the God of Abraham,* edited by Michael Bergmann et al., 85–89. Oxford: Oxford University Press, 2013.

De Bellafonds, Colleen. "When Does Your Baby Develop a Brain?" What to Expect, Jun. 22, 2021. https://www.whattoexpect.com/pregnancy/fetal-development/fetal-brain-nervous-system/.

Works Cited

Ehrman, Bart D. *Misquoting Jesus: The Story Behind Who Changed the Bible and Why.* New York: HarperCollins, 2005.

Episcopal Church. *The Book of Common Prayer and Administration of the Sacraments and Other Rites and Ceremonies of the Church: Together with the Psalter or Psalms of David According to the Use of the Episcopal Church.* New York: Seabury Press, 1979.

Evans, C. Stephen. *The Historical Christ and the Jesus of Faith: The Incarnational Narrative as History.* Oxford: Clarendon Press, 1996.

Gladwell, Malcolm. *The Bomber Mafia.* New York: Back Bay, 2021.

Gordon, Sherri. "Everything You Need to Know About Fetal Brain Development." Parents.com, Jun. 3, 2024. https://www.parents.com/when-does-a-fetus-develop-a-brain-8648531.

Green, Michael. *The Second Epistle General of Peter and the General Epistle of Jude: An Introduction and Commentary.* Grand Rapids: Eerdmans, 1987.

Henry, Carl F. "The Good as the Will of God." In *Introductory Readings in Ethics,* edited by William K. Frankena and John T. Granrose, 95–99. Englewood Cliffs, NJ: Prentice-Hall, 1974.

Herrick, Paul. *Philosophy, Reasoned Belief, and Faith: An Introduction.* Notre Dame, IN: University of Notre Dame Press, 2022.

Holden, Joseph M. and Norman Geisler. *The Popular Handbook of Archaeology and the Bible.* Eugene, OR: Harvest House, 2013.

Hopfe, Lewis M. *Religions of the World.* 4th ed. New York: Macmillan, 1987.

Kaiser, Walter C., Jr., et al. *Hard Sayings of the Bible.* Downers Grove, IL: IVP Academic, 1996.

The Koran. Translated by J. M. Rodwell. London: Orion, 1994. Originally published in 1861.

Layman, C. Stephen. *God: Eight Enduring Questions.* Notre Dame, IN: University of Notre Dame Press, 2022.

———. *Philosophical Approaches to Atonement, Incarnation, and the Trinity.* New York: Palgrave Macmillan, 2016.

LePage v. Mobile Infirmary Clinic, Inc. Supreme Court of the State of Alabama. SC–2022–515. Feb. 2024.

Lewis, C. S. *The Great Divorce.* London: Geoffrey Bles, 1945.

———. "Petitionary Prayer: A Problem Without an Answer." In C. S. Lewis, *Christian Reflections,* 142–51. Grand Rapids: Eerdmans, 1967.

———. "Why I Am Not a Pacifist." In C. S. Lewis, *The Weight of Glory and Other Addresses,* 33–53. New York: Macmillan, 1980.

Menssen, Sandra, and Thomas D. Sullivan. *The Agnostic Inquirer: Revelation from a Philosophical Standpoint.* Grand Rapids: Eerdmans, 2007.

Metzger, Bruce. "The Formation of the New Testament Canon." *Theology Matters* 1 (2014) 10–12.

Noonan, John T., Jr. "Abortion Is Not Morally Permissible." In *The Moral Life: An Introductory Reader in Ethics and Literature* (2nd ed.), edited by Louis P. Pojman, 789–96. New York: Oxford University Press, 2004.

Works Cited

Plantinga, Alvin. *Warranted Christian Belief.* New York: Oxford University Press, 2000.

Quran in English. Translated by Talal Itani. Dallas: ClearQuran, 2012.

Rowe, William. "The Problem of Evil and Some Varieties of Atheism." *American Philosophical Quarterly* 4 (1979) 335–41.

Royal College of Obstetricians and Gynecologists. "Fetal Awareness: Updated Review of Research and Recommendations." Dec. 2022. https://www.rcog.org.uk/guidance/browse-all-guidance/other-guidelines-and-reports/fetal-awareness-updated-review-of-research-and-recommendations-for-practice.

Sanders, Laura. "5 Misunderstandings of Pregnancy Biology That Cloud the Abortion Debate." *ScienceNews*, Jun. 24, 2022. https://www.sciencenews.org/article/abortion-roe-v-wade-pregnancy-biology-supreme-court-ruling.

Schellenberg, John. *Divine Hiddenness and Human Reason.* Ithaca, NY: Cornell University Press, 1993.

———. *Wisdom to Doubt: A Justification of Religious Skepticism.* Ithaca, NY: Cornell University Press, 2007.

Singer, Peter. *Practical Ethics.* New York: Cambridge University Press, 1979.

Smith, James E. *What the Bible Teaches About the Promised Messiah.* Nashville: Thomas Nelson, 1993.

Stark, Rodney. *Discovering God: The Origins of the Great Religions and the Evolution of Belief.* New York: HarperCollins, 2007.

Swinburne, Richard. *Revelation: From Metaphor to Analogy.* 2nd ed. Oxford: Oxford University Press, 2007.

———. "What Does the Old Testament Mean?" In *Divine Evil: The Moral Character of the God of Abraham*, edited by Michael Bergmann et al., 209–25. Oxford: Oxford University Press, 2013.

Tacitus. *The Annals of Imperial Rome.* Translated by Michael Grant. New York: Penguin, 1977.

Thomson, Judith Jarvis. "A Defense of Abortion." In *Vice and Virtue in Everyday Life: Introductory Readings in Ethics* (4th ed.), edited by Christina Sommers and Fred Sommers, 861–80. New York: Harcourt Brace, 1985.

Thucydides. *History of the Peloponnesian War.* Translated by Rex Warner. New York: Penguin, 1954.

Van Inwagen, Peter. "Comments on 'The God of Abraham, Isaac, and Jacob.'" In *Divine Evil: The Moral Character of the God of Abraham*, edited by Michael Bergmann et al., 79–84. Oxford: Oxford University Press, 2013.

Wasserman, Tommy. "Does the Woman Caught in Adultery Belong in the Bible?" Text and Canon Institute, Feb. 8, 2022. https://textandcanon.org/does-the-woman-caught-in-adultery-belong-in-the-bible.

Wielenberg, Erik J. "Omnipotence Again." *Faith and Philosophy* 1 (2000) 26–47.

Wolterstorff, Nicholas. *Divine Discourse: Philosophical Reflections on the Claim That God Speaks.* New York: Cambridge University Press, 1995.

———. *Justice in Love.* Grand Rapids: Eerdmans, 2015.

———. *Justice: Rights and Wrongs*. Princeton, NJ: Princeton University Press, 2008.

Wright, N. T. "Knowing Jesus: Faith and History." In *The Meaning of Jesus: Two Visions*, by Marcus Borg and N. T. Wright, 15–27. New York: HarperCollins, 1999.

Index

Abraham (patriarch), 15, 40, 66, 110
Abraham, William J., xi, 49–51
acorn-oak issue, 134, 137
adultery, 18, 62, 67, 110, 116
agapism, 32
aiōnion, 125
Alabama (Supreme Court of), 131
'almah, 84
almighty (defined), 7
animal sacrifice, 17, 36, 41, 46
annihilation, 23, 123
apostles, 104–8, 128–29
appropriated speech or writing, 2, 108
Augustine, 44–45

Barth, Karl, 28
blastocyst, 141
Blomberg, Craig, 97
brain death, 136–38
Bruce, F. F., 100, 103, 104–5
Brunner, Emil, 28

Caesar, 101
Canus lupus, 133
Chester Beatty Papyri, 101
child sacrifice, 36, 41, 66, 109
codex, 101

Codex Sinaiticus, 101
Codex Vaticanus, 101
Contextual Approach (to interpretation), 45–46, 47–48
creation chronology, 13
creationism, 138
Curley, Edwin, 27–29, 89

defeaters, 57–58
deputy (deputized speech or writing), 2, 108
Descartes, 56, 98
divine command theorists, 31
divine hiddenness (problem of), 8
divine justice, 15–16, 121–22
divine love, 8, 16, 120, 122–23
divinely inspired, 1
divorce, 67, 116

embryo, 131, 134–35, 138, 140–41
evil deity, 31
evil (problem of), 8, 111, 126

failed prophecy, 76, 79–80
fallible authorities, 2, 29, 103, 127–29
fetus, 132, 134, 136, 139
Fosdick, Harry Emerson, 28

Index

Gehenna, 119
genocide, 19–20, 36, 38–40, 44, 66, 109–11
Gregory of Nyssa, 44

harm principle, 114, 117–18
hell, 21, 26, 67, 119–26
hermeneutic of suspicion, 97–98, 128
Herrick, Paul, 136
Homo sapiens, 133–34
Human Author Approach (to interpretation), 42–43, 45, 47–48
human-life principle, 132–33, 135

image of God, 132, 135
incarnation, 4
Infallibilism, 29, 35, 41, 45
infallible, 1, 29, 77, 107, 127, 129
interpretation, 42
    Contextual Approach, 45–46, 47–48
    Human Author Approach, 42–43, 45, 47–48
    Sense of the Text Approach, 43
introspection, 56
Irenaeus, 44

James (apostle), 104
James (brother of Jesus), 115
John (apostle), 104

leadership roles (denied women), 25, 66, 116–17
Lewis, C. S., 123
lex talionis, 18, 23, 37, 63, 103, 110, 121–22

Maasi, 115
Menssen, Sandra, 10
Metzger, Bruce, 105

natural law theorists, 32

Neo-orthodox, 28
Neo-traditionalism, 29, 35, 41, 45

oculus contemplationis, 49–52
Origen, 44

parthenos, 84
Paul (apostle), 104–6
person, 135, 140–41
Peter (apostle), 104, 106, 115
Plantinga, Alvin, 53–56
potential, 140–42
predictive prophecy, 71
problem of divine hiddenness, 8
problem of evil, 8, 111, 126
properly basic beliefs, xi, 54–55, 57
prophecy (implicitly conditional), 77–78
psychic, 80

reductio ad absurdum, 27, 89
Reformed Epistemology, 53–54, 57, 59
respect principle, 114, 118
revelation, 1, 4–5, 60–61, 64–65, 68–70
role of women, 25, 66, 116–17
Roosevelt, Franklin D., 77

same-sex unions, 117–18
Schweitzer, Albert, 28
second coming, 24, 78
Sense of the Text Approach (to interpretation), 43
Septuagint, 84
slavery, 25, 66, 113–14
Smith, James E., 73, 75, 77, 83–84, 87
soon (second coming), 26, 79
soul, 136–39, 140–42
speciesism, 133
Stark, Rodney, 20, 50
suffering servant, 85–86
Sullivan, Thomas, 10

Index

Swinburne, Richard, 6, 44, 60, 64–65, 68–70

Tacitus, 101
theological voluntarists, 31
Thucydides, 96, 100–101
traducianism, 138

warrant, 54
whack-a-mole view (of hell), 122–23
Wolterstorff, Nicholas, 2, 122
Wright, N. T., 97

zygote, 134–35, 138, 140–41

www.ingramcontent.com/pod-product-compliance
Lightning Source LLC
Chambersburg PA
CBHW051107160426
43193CB00010B/1353